DATE DUE			
May 16 '77			
Jul 6 '77 D			
May 7 78			
Nov 9 0			

REVISED EDITION

A Guide to Movement Exploration

LAYNE C. HACKETT
San Jose City College
San Jose, California

ROBERT G. JENSON
Palo Alto Unified School District
Palo Alto, California

Photographs by
James Rand

PEEK PUBLICATIONS
4067 Transport Street
Palo Alto, California 94303

Sand
Top
Margin

Fore

Movement Exploration is ...roduce basic movement skills to pre-schoo ...ary grade children. It generates enthusiasm among children and provides continuous activity for all the children in a group. At the same time, Movement Exploration allows each child to progress at his own rate in a non-competitive, exhilirating learning situation that permits individual experimentation.

Many elementary school teachers who have witnessed demonstrations of this creative approach to teaching have requested information that will enable them to implement Movement Exploration in their physical education classes. The authors have written this book to meet the needs of those teachers. It has been written as a practical teaching guide, and an interested teacher (or parent) can effectively introduce a Movement Exploration program by following the procedures as outlined by the authors.

As an observer of this program in workshops and in actual classroom situations, it is my feeling that this approach to teaching basic motor skills will influence the teaching of primary physical education and will make a valuable contribution to elementary and secondary physical education methods.

Mel Stein
Coordinator of Physical Education
Santa Clara County Office of Education
San Jose, California

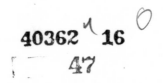

40362 16

47

Contents

Chapter I
Introduction to Movement Exploration

When we speak of movement exploration, we are talking about an approach to physical education. Movement is an integral part of physical education. It is considered one of the basic keys to learning. Children in the primary and intermediate years have an opportunity through movement to develop motor skills that will prepare them to progress to the various "readiness" stages.

This approach to physical education requires total physical and mental involvement. It is concerned with the whole body moving, exploring, seeking a solution to a stated problem. Because all children are simultaneously involved in the creative process, it may appear that there is a lack of discipline. This, however, is not so. The teacher, through some previously established controls, is always in command.

"When the whistle blows, stop, look and listen." The child responds naturally to this simple command. Since he is experiencing success, enthusiasm spontaneously rises and he listens eagerly for the next challenge. A child is never criticized for an incorrect response. For instance, if a child is challenged to hop but jumps instead, the teacher can point out a student who has responded correctly and ask him to demonstrate. Or the teacher can restate the challenge.

Research studies have indicated that many children entering kindergarten are deficient in basic learning functions, particularly motor skills. These skills are extremely vital. Movement exploration can provide a multitude of experiences to develop the child's motor potential and help him to live better in his cultural setting.

Movement begins at birth. A newborn child seeks to discover his new environment. Each movement contributes to his basic store of knowledge that can be recalled at a later date. Everything a child does from birth forward affects his performance in the future.

Movement exploration as an approach to physical education began in Europe, particularly Germany and England. A common underlying philosophy embraces both of these programs, that philosophy being that motor development is dependent upon numerous experiences involving all possible movement patterns. The German program, though creative, tends to be dependent upon specific physical skills. The British, perhaps the leaders in movement experiences, stress concepts of time, space, force and flow. [1] In a comparison of these two systems, the British may be more creative; but in any sense the basic theme is to know oneself better.

The movement program in America is by no means new. Many researchers have long known the relationship between motor development and achievement. However, under the impetus of psychology, we are now more than ever aware of motor-readiness relationships. For this reason there has been an emphasis on motor skills through movement exploration.

Many centers, as well as individuals, are now engaged in developing movement programs. Before long American children should be able to reap the benefits of an intensive program of movement.

One of the greatest values of movement exploration is the simplicity of the concept. Movement indicates that some action is used in seeking a solution to a problem. Each child is separately engaged in analyzing the problem and seeking a solution within the limitations of his own physical and mental abilities. By having to concentrate on the solution of a problem, rather than solely on himself, the child becomes completely involved in the lesson. There is little time to be critical of classmates. In spite of large classes, each child performs as an individual. The less skilled as well as the highly skilled are challenged. Each child experiences success.

Movement exploration requires a minimum of equipment and supplies. However, it is possible to extend the program to include the most elaborate facilities.

One of the main concerns of all physical educators is that a child is able to gain a sound background in motor development before he becomes engaged in activities that demand a high degree of proficiency. Through the development of motor skills, the child will be able to experience success as a participant in complex activities.

---

[1] Rudolf Laban and F. C. Lawrence, *Effort* (London, 1950)

Chapter II

The Program in Practice

One of the greatest values of movement exploration is the ease with which a teacher who may not be oriented toward physical education can present a sound program.

Besides the enthusiasm and general qualifications that are necessary for all successful teaching, [one who uses the movement exploration approach need only know the differences among certain basic motor skills and when a skill is being performed correctly] Such actions as jumping and hopping or jumping and leaping are different from one another, and dissimilarities must be recognized before any program in physical education can be competently taught. Beyond this skill vocabulary, however, [little or no special knowledge is expected of the teacher; and because teacher-demonstrations have no place in movement exploration, the teacher need not be an accomplished performer.]

GOALS

The goals of movement exploration are identical to those of any physical education program: [fitness, motor development, mental and social-emotional growth.] These, essentially, are the goals of education.

To implement movement exploration the teacher must first identify the activities the class needs to experience. These may be in the area of abdominal strength, agility or ball handling. Some of the activities must relate to fitness since this is a prime goal of physical education. Consequently, [activities stressing strength, endurance, flexibility, agility and balance should all be included in a variety of ways and through numerous movement problems throughout the school year.] It is essential to total fitness that each body part be used in as many demanding situations as possible. In movement exploration fitness results from the teacher's challenge to the child to respond in multiple movement patterns.

Motor development is a principal goal of physical education, but it is not unique to this field. Because gross motor skills are foundations on which more specific or dexterous movement patterns are established, all educators should be interested that each child receive the chance to develop large muscle control. The teacher of movement exploration, therefore, should include in the curriculum running, jumping and other locomotor skills as well as large muscle activities that relate to specific sports and games. The child who is deficient in these experiences will likely be disadvantaged in the classroom, and it is evident that children are being denied opportunities to explore movement outside of school.[1] In many cases boys and girls do not have the chance for extensive play experiences away from school. Because yards are too small for tumbling and streets are too dangerous for running, the child finds himself confined. Climbing trees may damage the tree, while to climb the neighbor's fence causes him to worry about liability. To get down on the ground may soil a pretty dress. In any case television is too fascinating and habit forming. As a result, many children are robbed of the experiences of creative play and vigorous activity. These experiences should be an integral part of every child's life. To encourage as many movement experiences as possible becomes the responsibility of the physical education teacher. The child who has a solid background in motor development will in turn be a more competent and a completely functioning human being.

To aid in the mental development of each child is most definitely a realistic goal of physical education. The fact that physical and mental development are very inter-related has been substantiated repeatedly. The quick, alert potential athlete is most often a child qualified for reaching a high academic standing. As one's physical abilities increase, he is better able to attain higher classroom standards.

In addition, if a child's confidence can be reinforced through any means, this confidence often is transferred into other areas of endeavor. The child who finds success on the physical education field, therefore, may gain in general confidence; and since movement exploration is developed upon successful experiences, it seems most conducive to increasing the child's self-esteem.

The glory of personal success and the strains of recognizing one's weaknesses are good tests of a child's emotional stability. Through movement exploration, the girl or boy learns two important things about himself: what he can do and what he cannot do. Because no class standard of performance is imposed upon the child, the way he solves a movement problem is not as important as the fact that he is successful. For this reason the child's capabilities are emphasized. Consequently, the child can accept his areas of weakness without feeling overwhelmed by failure or lack of ability. By experiencing multitudinous movement patterns and physical challenges, the child also realizes that he is neither best nor worst in every activity; rather these extreme positions are shared by everyone at one time or another.

Many activities in movement exploration are performed in groups or with a partner. Sometimes group planning or mutual agreement is required as part of the solution to a challenge. As an example: "How can you and your partner position yourselves so that one of you is the base and

---

[1] Newell C. Kephart, *The Slow Learner in the Classroom* (Columbus, 1964).

the other does not contact the ground?'' In problems such as these there are opportunities for social development. Leadership traits, democratic processes and general cooperation are encouraged. Of course, the age and sophistication of the class has considerable bearing on the amount of emphasis placed on group work, but most children perform surprisingly well in group situations.

IMPLEMENTATION OF GOALS

It can readily be noted that the goals of movement exploration parallel those of any good program in physical education. The uniqueness of movement exploration revolves around the approach and techniques used to attain these goals and the child's responses to the teacher's questions. Movement exploration involves seven steps, each of which is listed below and will be explained on the following pages:

- The teacher is to identify the particular movements and skills the child should experience.

- The movements and skills should be introduced in the form of a challenge which is geared for the level of the participant.

- The challenges should increase in difficulty in a logical progression both during the single class period and over a longer range of time.

- The teacher should phrase the question in a way that is specific enough for most of the responses to be anticipated and yet of sufficient latitude to encourage individual interpretation.

- Once the question is presented, the teacher should be able to distinguish between correct and incorrect responses.

- Individual interpretations of the challenges should be expected and encouraged.

- The teacher should strive to be creative and spontaneous in the presentation of the challenges.

IDENTIFICATION OF MOVEMENTS AND SKILLS

By knowing the goals of physical education the teacher is better able to make an educated selection of specific movements and general activities a class should experience. Since movement exploration is not a unit of physical education but a method of teaching, apparatus, stunts and tumbling, rhythms, work in skills and calisthenic-like activities are included via the method of movement exploration.

A good program will provide the child with opportunities in each of these areas and will work toward [applying these learned motor skills in game situations] To aid the teacher in identifying movements and skills that can be included in the movement exploration units he may organize several daily, weekly, and yearly lesson plans which can be found in the third chapter of this book.

√GEARING CHALLENGES TO PARTICIPANTS

[Motor development requires considerable repetition before perfection can be reached]. For this reason it is important that the teacher allow the child to repeat activities several times throughout a unit, the year, and even the six or seven years of elementary school. To do this in a way that is inspiring and challenging to the class the teacher must phrase the questions so that they are suitable to the particular group.

[Younger classes need ample opportunity to explore the many uses of their bodies. At this age questions should be rather simple and they should require only one or two skills at a given time] To use ball handling activities for an example: "Can you bounce the ball, keeping it waist high?" is sufficiently demanding of a beginning group. The skill of bouncing (called dribbling by older children) involves numerous subordinate skills. For instance, hand-eye coordination must be established to some degree. The child must accustom himself to the inflation level of the ball and must apply enough force to maintain a bounce height of waist level. The teacher will observe that the very young child, surprised at the springiness of the ball, will lose control of it; and in attempting to regain control, hit it harder and harder until it escapes him completely. The rebound surface must also be understood. A bumpy or slanted or soft surface will have a bearing on the ball's reaction. It can readily be seen, therefore, that the challenge, "Can you bounce the ball keeping it waist high?" is superficially elementary; but it is an appropriate challenge for a pre-schooler or first grader.

An older class, still in need of ball bouncing work, may respond more readily to a challenge that is geared more to its level. As an example "Who can dribble the ball in a manner that would allow an opponent the least opportunity for interception?" Essentially the same elements of skill are required of this class as were required of the younger children. In this case, however, the recommended height of rebound is not stated and must be estimated by the child. The fact that he is protecting the ball from an imaginary opponent may also cause him to adjust his body position accordingly.

There are only a certain number of separate movement patterns and skill combinations; and, in the final analysis, these skills can be performed in a limited number of ways unless they are creatively studied. [If the child is made to conform to a class standard of performance, the results are usually very predictable and restricting. For physical education to be exciting the child should be encouraged to exhaust his creative potential, attempting to explore movements from many different aspects] For instance, he should be motivated to interject moods into his performance in order to change the quality and give a new dimension to his actions. He might also explore the amplitude of force and its effects on the quality of movement.

It is important for the teacher to remember that [the level at which a challenge is geared can depend upon the emotional maturity, motor readiness, intelligence or general attitude of the class. It is not always determined solely upon the age factor] Of course, this is true in teaching in general.

PROGRESSIONS

(There are many kinds of progressions with which a teacher of physical education should be concerned. There is the order within the daily lesson plan as well as the overall yearly scheme. There is even the broad progression that should occur throughout the several years of elementary school)

In addition there are several subordinate progressions. Locomotor (transit) skills can best be learned in a simple to complex order. The concept of spatial awareness has a prescribed learning sequence also.

Sample daily and yearly lesson plans in movement exploration are provided in Chapter III of this book so that the teacher can use them or be guided in the programming of his own yearly unit. Logical progressions for locomotor skills are included within the yearly plans. If the teacher needs a more complete explanation of these, such information can be found in most texts of elementary school physical education.

The progression for spatial awareness is not frequently explained; yet it is crucial, for reasons of safety, that children know how to move among one another without colliding. The understanding of this progression will add to the teacher's confidence in planning a sound lesson.

(Four basic factors combine to form the concept of spatial awareness. These are area size, direction, speed and the number of participants) All movement requires space, and the complexity of a movement within or through that space is dependent upon the blending of these four points in several different combinations.

Where locomotor movements (movements that transport the body as a whole from one place to another) are involved, the size of the area in which the body can move affects the movement. It is easier to walk, run or leap in a large area than it is to perform these skills in a more confined spot. For this reason, [having unlimited space in which to move is the most elemental step in this aspect of spatial awareness while loco-motor movements performed in a smaller area require greater skill.

When more than one participant is involved in an activity, the direction of traffic affects the difficulty of the activity. Moving en masse in one direction is the simplest and safest step. If the direction is forward, there is even less danger of accident since everyone can see the path he is taking. To move as a group but in a direction other than forward compounds the difficulty of the activity. The ultimate degree of difficulty is for all participants to move in any direction they desire and to change that direction whenever they wish. In this case, not only must each child decide on the path he wants to follow, but he must anticipate the actions of every other participant.

The progression in speed moves from slow to fast. In spatial awareness, therefore, the simplest activities involving group movement are performed walking. Later the tempo advances to a fast walk and continues to increase until all children are running at a speed that remains just within the threshold of their individual control levels.

The final factor in spatial awareness involves the size of the group. In a sense the size of the group and area size are related. The more bodies that occupy a given space, the less vacant space remains. The number of participants is significant in another way, however. Each performer moving through space is an obstacle to all other members of the group. For every additional participant, the child must anticipate more dodges, changes in speed, stops and starts.

For the teacher who is aiding a group in this very important area of spatial awareness, a brief explanation of progressions may be useful. Since all locomotor movement involves the four above factors, to explore the combination at its simplest level would be the first step. As an example, for a small number of children to walk forward in a large area would be rather simple. Ultimately a larger group, having progressed in a logical order, should be able to cope with the problem of moving in all possible directions within a confined space at a high rate of speed.

PHRASING OF QUESTIONS

One of the most important techniques of movement exploration is the phrasing of the questions or challenges. The challenge is the medium through which movement exploration is conducted. If the teacher is not constantly aware of how the questions sound and how they may be interpreted, much will be lost.

It is essential that the teacher speak literally. In other words, the teacher must always mean exactly what he says. Although this may sound ridiculously simple and superfluous, it is amazing how often one misstates an intended challenge.

Before a challenge is formed, the teacher should know the approximate responses he expects to draw from the class. The question must then be stated clearly.

If the question, "Who can jump over the bench?" is asked, the teacher should have a pre-conceived idea of the general kinds of responses the children may give. He can assume that no child will attempt to dive over the bench because the task was to jump the obstacle. For the same reason, the teacher can be quite positive that no child will come to rest on top of the bench. If the challenge had been, "Find a way to go over the bench," then either diving or coming to rest on the bench before landing on the far side would be as correct as jumping.

The teacher should be able to recognize correct responses from those that are incorrect. Although individual interpretation is encouraged in movement exploration and the teacher should avoid setting class standards of achievement, movement skills have specific labels which the child should learn. If, when challenged to jump, a child leaps, his response is incorrect. If he is asked to bounce the ball but instead strikes it in a direction other than downward, again the response is incorrect. Teachers who use skill terminology indiscriminately should be particularly careful in this aspect of question phrasing.

Sometimes it is desirable to limit a challenge or make it rather specific. This depends on the objectives involved in the particular task. If abdominal strength is the objective, the child must be challenged to perform a rather specific action, such as, "Can you balance on just your seat, keeping your knees straight and toes pointed?" It is possible to balance on the seat with knees bent and with the child's arms around his lower legs, but the need for abdominal strength is removed.

In contrast to the above example, many challenges are very general. "In how many different positions can you balance on a two point base?" is a problem that can challenge the most active imagination. Similarly, "Find a new way to move from your home base to the wall and back. Change levels at least once," can stimulate a variety of creative responses.

To aid the teacher in his first attempts at phrasing questions in movement exploration, specific daily lesson plans and additional sample questions are provided. The talent for stating the challenge is the single most important technique of movement exploration, but it is not difficult to master.

EVALUATION OF RESPONSES

It was mentioned previously that the teacher should strive to be exact in forming challenges, and the child should be trained to interpret the teacher literally. If a child responds to a challenge with an incorrect skill, first the teacher should reconsider what he has said. If the challenge was phrased precisely and the child misinterpreted it, then the child should be corrected by having the challenge re-emphasized. If the teacher found that the challenge was misstated, the child cannot be considered incorrect. In this case, the problem must be rephrased.

Because movement exploration is intended to help improve the child's self-image, correcting an incorrect response should be handled in a positive manner. In movement exploration, children very seldom deliberately perform incorrectly; so rephrasing the challenge is a more effective correcting technique than reprimanding.

Evaluation is a constant responsibility of a teacher in any subject area. Movement exploration is no exception. Here, however, the teacher's first concern is quantitative rather than qualitative. How many different tasks can the child solve is the foremost question. How skillfully he performs the solution is important, but secondary. Once it is established that the child can perform a particular movement such as a vertical jump, the teacher can work toward a more qualitative response by encouraging greater height, a softer landing, or a generally more efficient movement pattern. Again, however, this more refined performance is the result of challenges in movement, rather than a demonstration or specific instruction. "Many of you are using just your legs while jumping. Experiment to see if your arms can help you reach a greater height," is an example of how skill can be improved.

It has already been emphasized that there is no class standard of achievement, no uniform method of performing in movement exploration. A child's unique manner of solving a problem is not only accepted; it is encouraged at every opportunity. It is the intent of movement exploration that each child know as much about himself and his physical abilities and limitations as possible. The goal is for the task to be solved in a way suitable to the individual, but for the individual to continually strive for better performance.

Children are delightfully imaginative in creative settings and far less inhibited than the adult leader. For the teacher to attempt to influence the child's interpretation of a problem by demonstrating or insisting that the boy or girl's response is too extreme defeats the entire purpose of exploring movement and should be totally discouraged.

TEACHER CREATIVITY

There is a definite place for teacher creativity in movement exploration. The teacher who will be most successful in teaching via this method is one who is willing to venture into new ideas. He can complement a program that may otherwise be mediocre, for instance by being inventive with improvised equipment. To teach a unit based on a theme through movement exploration also can open the doors to exciting movement experiences. The possibilities and needs for the teacher to tap every creative resource at his command cannot be overemphasized.

TEACHING TECHNIQUES FOR MOVEMENT EXPLORATION

Possibly the most threatening aspect of attempting movement exploration for the first time is the fact that the concept is somewhat new and different from the way the teacher has previously taught physical education. Even if he sees merit in the concept, the first few attempts in teaching may seem somewhat formidable. For this reason a few techniques that may aid the teacher in his initial experiences in movement exploration are described on the following pages.

CLASS FORMATIONS

The organization of a class is one of the teacher's first considerations. It is traditional that physical education be taught from lines, circles and other pre-arranged formations. This is understandable when the children are expected to wait for turns to perform. Lines also provide an external control on rambunctious youngsters. In movement exploration, however, the most common formation is one which is scattered. Because all children are active simultaneously the majority of the time, there is very little need to take turns. The only considerations are that each child have enough room to move comfortably and that each child be able to hear the teacher. "Spread out," is the term used in positioning the children for participation. This scattered formation is consistent with the expressiveness of movement exploration. It is difficult to move individually and creatively if a line keeps one in uniform proximity with other members of the class.

SIGNALS

The very first responsibility the teacher has in proceeding with his class is to establish certain signals and to be sure that they are understood. It is recommended that the whistle be consistently used for only one signal: that is, to STOP, LOOK and LISTEN. It can be used indoors and out of doors, of course, at varying volumes. If the teacher begins to interchange signals, such as hand clapping for stopping or the whistle to begin running, the class becomes confused and does not respond as satisfactorily. Because the class is usually quiet and waiting for the signal to begin an activity, the verbal command, "go," is sufficient.

Hand or body signs are very important in physical education for reasons of safety. Young children often are confused by direction. Until they can move at random among their classmates without colliding, it is important for all children to move in the same direction. A body signal accompanied by a voice command is the best guarantee against accidents. If the class is to move in a counter-clockwise circle, the teacher should explain this in two ways. "Boys and girls, run in a big circle going THIS way." On "THIS," the teacher sweeps his hand and turns his body in a wide counter-clockwise arc. As he does this, he watches to be sure that he has the attention of each child. Then he says, "go".

QUESTION PHRASING

Much has already been said about the phrasing of challenges in movement exploration. A short discussion of some of the lead-in phrases may aid the teacher, however. Most challenges are introduced by one of the following phrases: "Who can . . . ," "Can you . . . ," "What can . . . ," "How can . . . ," or "Show me . . ." "Can you find a new way to roll?" "What can you do on the horizontal ladder that takes a great deal of strength?

TERM OF PRACTICE

During the teacher's first few lessons in movement exploration, it is sometimes confusing to determine how long the class should be permitted to explore a particular problem. The children's responses are the best barometer for gauging the length of an activity. If the problem is strenuous such as "How high can you jump?" or "Can you run quickly, changing directions on signal?" the children will show fatigue and should be allowed to explore for only a few minutes. If the challenge requires a lesser output of energy, it can be explored for several minutes. This is especially true during a unit of rhythms when a group of children may be arranging different movements to a rhythmic pattern. The teacher quickly learns to read fatigue symptoms and interest levels and can regulate the vigorousness of a lesson accordingly.

SAFETY

Teachers first introduced to movement exploration often inquire about the safety of a program that allows children to attempt physical feats not allowed under other circumstances. Seemingly so much expressive activity during which everyone is involved and often moving among one another at high rates of speed would be conducive to accidents.

To the contrary, movement exploration has proved to be a very safe form of physical education. Possibly the key reasons for this are individual interpretation and individual standards of achievement. The child is expected and encouraged to do his best but not to compete with other members of the class. Also, the fact that much time is spent in developing spatial awareness has considerable bearing on the high safety record of the program. In addition, however, there is a subtlety related to the phrasing of challenges that may influence safety. The question, "How high can you climb up the rope?" as opposed to "Climb the rope until you are even with that mark on the wall", demonstrates that no uniform goal is given to the class as a whole. For this reason, the child does not have to fear that he cannot meet the set standard; and, consequently, he is less apt to overtax himself. Conversely, the child who is capable of performing safely at a level above the other children is not frustrated by an objective which is too elementary.

DEMONSTRATIONS

One of the advantages of movement exploration for the classroom teacher is that there is no place for teacher demonstration. Consequently, he need not be a skilled performer. This should be emphasized because one of the most common mistakes made by a teacher first experimenting with this method is to substitute demonstrations for skillful challenge phrasing. For the teacher to demonstrate lessens the child's opportunity to be imaginative in his responses. In addition, demonstrations remove the need for the boy or girl to interpret the challenge and to be a good listener.

The teacher who finds himself attempting to demonstrate should evaluate his ability to form concise challenges and spend time practicing the phrasing of problems. His efforts will be rewarded by a more imaginative and less restricted class.

Occasionally there is an appropriate time for demonstrations by a class member. Usually to demonstrate is a reward for outstanding performance or exceptional self-discipline. The highly skilled or creative child can show his interpretation and possibly the class can practice what the child demonstrates. At other times, the child who is not particularly capable in motor skills will have one exceptionally good idea. This should be his opportunity to be in the limelight. Still on other occasions, the boy or girl who is generally a discipline problem can be rewarded for outstanding self-control by demonstrating the challenge he solved while on good behavior. Without exception, however, a demonstration **follows** the class' opportunity to answer the challenge, and the demonstrator must honestly deserve the moment.

DISCIPLINE

Because movement exploration is exciting, quick moving and challenging, discipline is rarely a problem. Some minor conditions that may make class control difficult can be avoided by a few simple techniques.

Whenever equipment is being passed out to the class, the boys and girls are anxious to know if there will be enough for every participant. Consequently, there is a rush to be the first supplied. Merely to explain the amount of available equipment and whether there will be partners who share or small groups or individuals each supplied is very important to the child. Knowing that his position in line will not determine his chances for being provided a piece of equipment makes him less of a discipline problem.

Confusion and teacher frustration can be avoided if the teacher presents a challenge to be undertaken as soon as the individual boy or girl gets the necessary equipment. "When you are given a ball, take it on the black top and practice bouncing it while keeping your feet stationary." It is unnatural to expect any boy or girl to hold something as exciting as a ball until the entire class is supplied. In any case, the few seconds of practice available to the children at times such as these can amount significantly. Likewise, when returning equipment to the supply area, the children can be given a task to perform en route. For instance, "Who can skip rope from where you are to the jump rope bag?" Some child is going to skip rope to the equipment area even if the directions are to "walk quietly". It seems unnecessary for him to be labeled a discipline problem just because he wants more practice.

SUMMARY

Having read the above explanations of movement exploration and by using the sample lesson plans provided in Chapter III, the teacher should now be ready to experiment with this concept. It is important to remember that [the teacher's individual personality is part of the vitality of the program and that his individual identity should be retained.] Much of what he does in teaching through this approach may differ from the description in this book, but is is through creative teaching that the idea of movement exploration can be expanded. Each teacher venturing into the program will undoubtedly see responses from children that no one else has witnessed. In turn, he will probably challenge his students in novel ways. This spontaneity and eagerness to explore the potentials of movement exploration are the very factors that make the exploration of movement exciting.

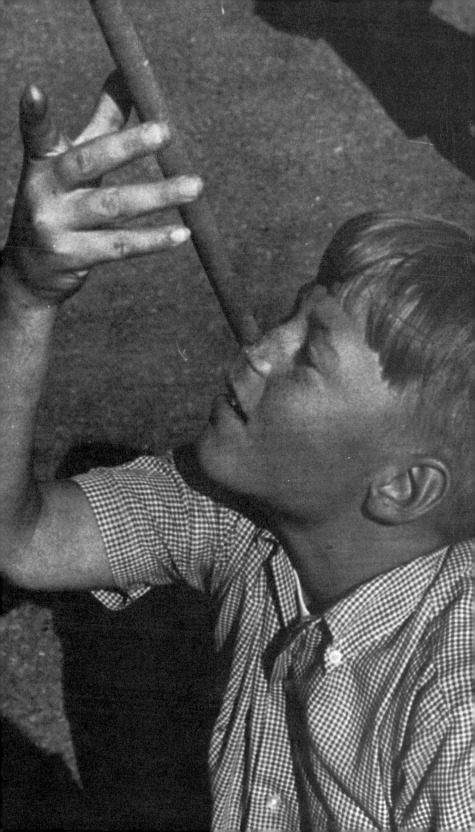

Chapter III
Questions and Challenges

The following section contains sample questions. They are the suggested progressive steps in building a program in movement exploration. Depending on the age level of the class, it may be necessary to modify the phrasing of the question.

LOCOMOTOR ACTIVITIES

Walking

1. Walking among classmates who are confined to a relatively large area.
2. Can you decrease the size of the area and walk among classmates?
3. Avoid all personal contact while walking among classmates in a defined area.
4. Take as few steps as possible to move from one place to another.
5. Who can walk quickly and quietly?
6. While walking, change direction on signal.
7. Change direction but remain facing in same direction.
8. Can you walk gayly?
9. Feel angry while walking.
10. On signal change levels (height) while walking.
11. Change level and direction while walking.
12. Keep hands low while walking at a high level.
13. Keep the hands high while walking at a low level.
14. Can you change levels while walking but keep one part of the body at a constant level?
15. Repeat activity # 14, but this time keep another part of the body at a constant level.
16. Express your mood while walking. Is it happy, frightened, tired?
17. Walk in a circle while moving from one point to another.
18. Draw a pattern on a large piece of paper and walk that pattern.
19. Walk a pattern; then draw it on a large piece of paper.

20.   Show me how a person walks on a rainy day?

21.   What would a person look like walking on an icy day?

22.   How would wind affect the way a person walks?

Running

1.   Can you run among classmates within a large area avoiding personal contact?

2.   Repeat # 1 narrowing the given area.

3.   Repeat # 1 again narrowing the area as much as is reasonable.

4.   Run and stop on signal.

5.   See how quickly you can stop running when the signal is given.

6.   Run and change direction on the signal.

7.   Run to a specific point and return to original position.

8.   Take as few running steps as possible to get from one point to another.

9.   Run as quietly as possible.

10.   Can you start very low and eventually reach the highest possible running position?

11.   Starting very low, run as quickly as possible to a given point.

12.   Run repeatedly to the count of ten, each time going farther than the time before.

13.   On a piece of paper draw many connected straight lines and run this pattern.

14.   Run a pattern different from any run before. Then draw this pattern on a piece of paper.

Jumping

1.   How can you jump as high as possible?

2.   Repeat, jumping high but landing quietly.

3.   Jump and turn around as far as possible.

4.   Jump as far as possible from a stationary start.

5.   Run and jump as far as possible.

6.   Repeat # 5 landing quietly.

7.   Jump and while in the air move some part of the body in a striking action.

8.   Jump backward.

9. Jump sideways.
10. Can you do something different from before at the height of the jump?
11. Jump and bring both feet forward; recover and land.
12. Jump and take both feet backward; recover and land.

Hopping

1. Hop on first one foot and then the other.
2. Repeat #1, hopping quietly.
3. Hop for height.
4. Hop for distance.
5. Who can hop in different directions?
6. Change the level of the upper body while hopping.
7. At the height of the hop make some striking motion.

Sliding

1. Slide forward.
2. See if you can slide backward.
3. Slide to the side.
4. Slide in any direction, changing directions in order to avoid a collision.
5. Can you move in long sliding movements?
6. While sliding, try something never tried before.
7. While sliding, change the body level.
8. What else can be done while sliding?
9. Find a partner and slide while holding his hand.
10. Try sliding face to face with the partner.
11. Try sliding back to back with the partner.
12. Is it possible to slide face to face then back to back without stopping?
13. How else can partners slide together?
14. Slide around a stationary partner; then exchange places.
15. What else can be done while sliding with partner?
16. Take another partner (making a group of three), and slide.
17. Find a way to slide as a group in a circle.

18.   In what other patterns can a trio slide?

19.   Can one of the partners slide in a large triangle around the other two partners who are sliding in a circle?

20.   Now make up a new sliding pattern within the trio.

Skipping

1.   Practice skipping while moving in a particular direction.

2.   Skip among classmates, changing directions in order to avoid collisions.

3.   Skip as lightly as possible.

4.   Lift as high off the ground as possible while skipping.

5.   Try something new while skipping.

6.   Do something different with the hands while skipping.

7.   Lean from the waist—first to one side, then to the other—while skipping.

8.   Skip backward.

9.   Narrow the action area. Now skip among the classmates avoiding personal contact.

10.   Skip in a square.

11.   Skip in your own circle.

12.   How can you skip in many directions while facing only in one of two directions?

13.   Take a few skips as possible to get from one point to another.

14.   Skip as quickly as possible from one point to another.

Leaping

1.   What is a leap?

2.   Leap many times in any direction avoiding a collision.

3.   Take as few leaps as possible to get from one point to another.

4.   Change the position of the arms at the height of the leap.

5.   Lift the arms as high as possible at the height of the leap.

6.   Leap with the same arm and leg forward.

7.   Leap with the opposite arm and leg forward.

8.   Which way is more comfortable?

9.   With a partner leap toward a certain point.

10. Can one partner move in a different way while the partner is leaping?

11. Leap as high into the air as possible.

12. Lift the legs higher when leaping this time.

13. Can three partners leap together while holding hands?

14. Can the middle partner run while the side partners are leaping?

15. Can the side partners run while the middle partner is leaping?

16. In what other patterns can three partners leap?

General Locomotion

1. Notice where you are standing.

2. Move away from the home spot; then return when the signal "home" is given.

3. Move farther away from "home" again returning on signal.

4. Move farther away from "home" and look in another direction. Return on signal.

5. Look around to avoid collisions. Run about the room, returning "home" on signal.

6. Look at a spot away from home. Go to that spot as quickly as possible; then return home.

7. This time find two spots away from home. Visit one spot and then the other, returning home as quickly as possible.

8. Move in this (arm signal) direction in the fastest method you can.

9. Return home quickly.

10. In a low position, move from that direction (signal) until the whistle blows. Come back home in another low position.

11. Find a way to get from here to there (gesture), moving from high to low, high to low many times.

12. Again move high to low in this (signal) direction, but do not leave the ground.

13. What can you do that will cause one side to lead as you move from here to there (gesture)?

14. Come back with the other side leading.

15. Find a place where you have a great deal of room to yourself. Move about that space in the pattern of a large "O".

16. Move in a pattern that will form this (flash card) shape (square).

17.   Can you move backward in that same pattern?

18.   Is it possible to face in one direction while moving in the square pattern?

19.   Now try to move in the pattern of this shape (triangle).

20.   Who can move in the pattern of a letter "C"?

21.   Without moving from the spot where you are standing, can you again move in the pattern of a "C"?

22.   Is it possible to move in the pattern of a "Z"?

23.   How could you move in the pattern of an "X", touching the ground only where you would want to leave a line?

24.   Now make an "X" with your body while standing where you are.

25.   Can you make a pattern of the first letter in your first name?

26.   Try moving backward while making the pattern of the letter of your last name.

27.   How would your full first name look if you moved in a pattern to form all of the letters?

28.   What other words can you spell through movement?

29.   Can you walk in the pattern of the word "walk"?

30.   Can you run in the pattern of the word "run"?

31.   Let's try to skip the pattern of the word "skip".

APPARATUS

Horizontal Ladder—Parazontal Bars

1.   Can you go hand over hand on the rungs?

2.   Who can travel sidways on the single rail?

3.   Who can go hand over hand on both outside rails?

4.   Can you go across the ladder with your legs in a sitting position?

5.   When you meet another person coming across, find a way to pass him. (Start from both sides with double rail single rail.)

6.   Find a way to go across the ladder using two feet and two hands.

7.   Can you go across some way you have never gone before?

8.   Who can hang for 20 seconds? . . . 30 seconds?

Horizontal Bar

1.   Can you hang from the bar with just your knees?

2.   Who can place his knee over the bar and make a circle forward and then one backward?

3.   While hanging from your knees, can you swing up to catch the bar?

Turning Bars (Low - High)

1.   Who can turn himself over the bar? (pancake flip)
2.   Can you pull yourself under the bar and then over the top?
3.   Can you place one leg over the bar and turn several times?
4.   Who can go over backwards with one leg over the bar?
5.   Can you jump to the bar with just your stomach touching?

Ladder (Inclined Position)

1.   Can you go up the ladder using your hands and feet?
2.   In what other way can you use your hands and feet to go up the ladder?
3.   Can you weave in and out of the rungs?
4.   Can you go up the ladder without touching the rungs?
5.   Who can use just his feet to go up the ladder?
6.   This time while using your feet can you touch every rung?
7.   Can you skip every other rung?
8.   Who can go down the ladder using his hands and feet?
9.   Can you go down head first?
10.   Can you go down feet first?
11.   Can you walk down each rung?
12.   Can you walk backward down each rung?
13.   How else can you get from one end of the ladder to the other?

Ladder (Horizontal Position Resting on Two Saw Horses)

1-13.   Same as above.
14.   Who can go along the underneath side of the ladder?
15.   Can you do this without touching the ground?
16.   Can you go feet first?
17.   Let's try moving head first along the underneath side.

Tables (Picnic)

1.   Get on the table. Run across and jump off.
2.   This time when you jump off, can you clear this obstacle? (The stick is held by the teacher.)

3. How far can you jump when you leave the table?

4. Find a new way to get on the table.

5. Can you do a stunt on the table?

6. Get on the table in a new way, run, jump off and roll after you land.

7. Can you roll across the table?

8. Can you go across the table on your stomach and dismount from that position?

9. Who can get on the table without using his hands?

10. Can you touch your heels when jumping off the table?

Hurdles (Wooden Blocks Bridged by a Wooden Dowel that Can Easily Fall Off if Knocked; Hurdles Can Vary in Height)

1. Who can run and clear all of the hurdles?

2. If you were successful, see if you can do it again. If you missed some of the hurdles, try to improve.

3. Who can jump each hurdle?

4. Now can you leap each hurdle?

5. How fast can you clear the hurdles? (Count or use stop watch, adding five seconds for each downed hurdle.)

6. This time can you beat your best hurdle time record?

Stairs (See Appendix for Diagram — If More Than One Set, Place in Row)

1. Can you go across the stairs touching every one quickly?

2. Who can hop up and down the stairs, touching the rails only for balance?

3. Repeat that on the other foot.

4. How can you go across the stairs touching just the lowest and highest steps?

5. Can you weave in and out of the uprights?

6. This time go under the rails through the first uprights, over the rails at the next uprights, and continue to alternate.

7. How far can you go across the stairs without touching a single step?

8. Can you do that again moving backward?

9. Find another way to cross the stairs without touching the steps.

Balance Board (3 Bases — 5 x 5, 4 x 4, 3 x 3)

1. Can you look at this object while balancing?
2. Who can bounce the ball in front of him and catch it? Can you bounce with the other hand?
3. Can you bounce it more than once without having to catch it?
4. Can you throw the ball and hit a target?
5. Who can touch his feet and get back up without losing balance?
6. Find other ways to move and still keep your balance.
7. While balancing can you touch your shoulders? . . . knees? . . . toes? . . . head? . . . hips?
8. Who can touch his left knee with his right hand. (Continue to give opposite identifications.)
9. Can you balance on one foot? (return) Can you balance on the other?
10. Can you jump up and still keep your balance?
11. Can you jump the rope while balancing?
12. Can you stand tall? Can you go down low?

Walking Board — Balance Beam

1. Who can walk slowly across the board touching heel against toe?
2. Can you go across the board backward while touching heel against toe?
3. Can you cross backward and not look at your feet?
4. Who can cross the board moving slowly sideways?
5. Can you walk across the board, turn without stepping off, and walk back sideways?
6. Who can cross to the middle, stop, bounce and then go on?
7. Can you go just halfway, turn and come back?
8. How many steps do you need to go across the board? Can you count them?

EQUIPMENT

Ball Handling

1. Can you bounce the ball keeping it waist high?
2. Now can you take the ball down to a very low bounce?
3. Can you change hands and keep the ball bouncing just as low with this hand?

4. This time, how low can YOU go while bouncing the ball? Keep it bouncing as you get into that low position.

5. Bounce to a standing position and repeat this with the other hand.

6. Can you go down lower while bouncing with this second hand?

7. Come to a standing position again while bouncing the ball.

8. Try bouncing the ball while looking away from the ball. Try not to peek.

9. Change hands many times while doing this.

10. Can you bounce the ball very low while doing this?

11. Now can you move among your friends without bumping, while bouncing the ball? You may have to look around now and then to avoid bumping.

12. Change hands many times while doing this.

13. Who can bounce the ball with a different part of the body? Remember that to bounce the ball means to strike it downward.

14. Find another part of the body with which you can bounce the ball.

15. Can you bound the ball into the ground and catch it before it bounces again?

16. Try this many times.

17. Now can you bound the ball into the ground and jump to catch it before it bounces again?

18. How high can you toss the ball, catching it before it bounces?

19. If you are successful, try to toss it even higher.

20. Place the ball on the ground. Find a way to go over the ball without touching it.

21. Try this several times, changing the way you go over the ball each time.

22. How can you get the ball from your feet to your partner's hands?

23. Can you find another way to get the ball from your feet to your partner's hands.

24. Show me if you can volley the ball with your hands many times.

25. Count the most number of times that you can volley the ball in succession.

26. Now try to volley the ball with different parts of your body, using your hands only when it is necessary to regain control of the ball.

27.   Place the ball on the ground and gently kick it with the inside of one foot then the inside of the other foot. Try to keep the ball quite close to you at all times. Walk as you do this.

28.   Repeat this, walking faster if you can. Look up to see where you are going.

29.   If you have been able to keep the ball quite close to you while dribbling with your feet, practice dribbling while running.

30.   Throw the ball down the field, retrieve it and sit down.

31.   Now throw it back this way and retrieve it.

32.   Try to kick the ball straight ahead of you down the field. Retrieve it and sit down.

33.   Do the same thing coming back this way.

Hula Hoops

1.   Can you roll your hoop and keep it from falling over?

2.   While it is rolling, can you make it turn without having to stop it?

3.   Who can spin his hoop like an egg beater?

4.   How can you throw the hoop on the ground so that it will return to you? (Try several ways.)

5.   Can you throw the hoop high in the air and catch it before it lands?

6.   While rolling your hoop, can you jump through it?

7.   Can you climb in and out and around your hoop?

8.   Who can make the hoop turn circles while it is on his arm?
        . . . while it is around his neck?
        . . . while it is around his foot?

9.   While holding the hoop, can you use it as a jumping rope?

10.   Who can jump into a hoop held by his partner? Let your partner try.

11.   Can you and your partner throw a hoop back and forth to each other?

12.   Find some different ways to get it to your partner.

13.   See if you can throw your hoop so that your partner is in the middle of it.

Batons (Wands)

1.   Can you balance your baton on the ground, turn around once, and catch it before it falls.

2.   Who can balance the baton on the palm of his hand? . . . two fingers? . . . one finger?

3.   Balance the baton in a new way.

4.   While balancing the baton, can you move down low? . . . come back up high?

5.   Can you turn around while balancing the baton?

6.   Can you drop the baton, let it bounce, and catch it while it is still in the air?

7.   Holding the baton at both ends, can you step over it?

8.   While sitting, hold baton at both ends and pass under lifted legs.

9.   Can you balance the baton on your foot?

10.   Can you balance the baton on your chin.

Tires (Individual)

1.   Who can run around his tire?

2.   Can you go the other way?

3.   How else can you move around the tire?

4.   Can you put one foot in the middle of the tire as you jump over it?

5.   Can you carefully put both feet in the middle of the tire as you jump across?

6.   Can you jump and touch both sides of the tire as you miss the middle?

7.   Can you jump on and then bounce off?

8.   Find some other things you can do.

Tires — Several in Sequence

1.   Who can run quickly through all the tires without touching?

2.   Let's skip back the same way you came. Be certain not to touch the tires.

3.   Can you run through the tires and put your foot in the middle of each one?

4.   Think of some new way to go through the tire course.

Stilts

1.   Who can place both feet on the stilts and balance for three counts?

2.   Can you balance for more than three counts? Try.

3.   Now can you take one step?

4. Who can take two steps before dismounting?

5. See if each time you attempt walking you can increase the number of steps.

6. Now can you walk backward?

7. Who can cross his feet over as he steps sideways?

8. Go to the blacktop. Can you walk along the painted lines without going off course?

9. Go to the hop scotch area. Can you walk the hop scotch course by putting one stilt in each square?

10. Try that coming back along the course.

11. How long can you balance on one stilt before placing the other one on the ground?

12. Can you step onto the stair, then down again?

Jump Ropes

1. With the rope laid in a straight line on the floor, can you walk it as if it were a tight rope?

2. Can you do this while moving backward?

3. Who can walk the "tightrope" with his eyes shut?

4. Can you jump from side to side across the rope without touching the rope?

5. Show me if you can hop from side to side without touching the rope.

6. How else can you move along the rope, using your feet, without touching the rope? Try a new idea each time.

7. Can you straddle the rope, jump into the air, turn around and land on your feet straddling the rope?

8. How far around can you spin still landing on your feet and straddling the rope?

9. Can you criss-cross your hands and feet without touching the rope as you move along it?

10. Can you do this while moving backward?

11. What other movement pattern can you invent in which you use your hands and feet while moving along the rope without touching it?

12. Lay your rope in the pattern of a circle. Can you get inside the circle, taking up as much space as possible without hanging over the edges?

13.   In what other position can you solve this problem?

14.   Can you solve this problem while touching the ground with five parts of your body?

15.   Make several little circles with your rope. Can you put one body part in each circle and balance?

16.   'Can you do this while using body parts you didn't use last time?

17.   Pick up the rope. While I count to fifteen, how many times can you jump rope?

18.   Remember the number of times you were able to jump rope. Let's try it again and see if you can beat your old record.

19.   Watching out for the people around you, can you jump rope while moving in many directions throughout the room?

20.   To "jump rope" means to use two feet at the same time. Can you hop rope?

21.   In how many other ways can you go through the spinning rope?

22.   With your rope, make the first letter of your first name. Can you shape yourself into that same shape?

23.   Do the same thing with the first letter of your last name. Can you walk the tightrope of this pattern?

24.   If your rope were shaped as the letter "V," could you jump over the "V" without touching the rope?

25.   See how close you can come to jumping or leaping over the widest part of the "V."

FLASH CARDS

Circle (Hold up Circular Flash Card)

1.   Who can move in a small circle?

2.   Can you make the circle larger?

3.   Can you move backward in the circle?

4.   Keep one part of your body stationary and rotate around that point.

5.   Can you move in a circle using a different pivot point?

6.   Move in the circular pattern and change levels (high to low or low to high) on signal.

7.   Can you run in a circle?

8.   What else can you do in a circular pattern?

9.   What other kind of circular movement can you make?

10.   Can you make a circle using just one part of your body?

11.   Now can you make several circles at one time?

12.   How many parts of your body will move in a circle?

Square (Present Square Flash Card)

1.   Who can walk in this pattern?

2.   Can you run in this pattern?

3.   Each time you reach a corner, do a different locomotor skill.

4.   When you change direction, can you change levels?

5.   Can you change direction, levels and locomotor steps all at once?

6.   Who can move in a square while facing one direction?

Rectangle

1.   Same as for square.

Triangle

1.   Same as for square.

"X"

1.   Can you move in this pattern?

2.   Who can find a way to move in the "X" without retracing his steps?

3.   Is there another way to solve the problem?

4.   How else can you make the shape of an "X"?

Letters and Words

1.   Who can walk the letter pattern "V"?

2.   What is the first letter of your first name? Can you walk that letter pattern?

3.   Now can you walk the letter pattern of your last name?

4.   Who can walk the word pattern of his first name?

5.   Show me if you can walk the word "walk".

6.   Can you hop the word "hop"?

7.   . . . jump the word "jump"?

8.   . . . run the word "run"?

9.   Who can write a word on his piece of paper and then walk that same word pattern?

10.   Now move anywhere you want, but remember each direction you take.

11.   Now draw that pattern on your paper.

12.   Can you draw a new pattern then move to it?

13.   How do you feel? Happy? Tired? Afraid?

14.   Move around in whatever mood you feel.

15.   Draw the pattern on your paper and now color the drawing in a way to tell your mood.

IDEAS FOR RHYTHMIC THEMES

[In presenting rhythms to children it is important that a logical progression be developed so that the child can understand and feel the basic rhythmic pattern before he is expected to incorporate this pattern at an advanced level. A progression that has worked successfully and is recommended in the teaching of rhythms is outlined below:

1.   Present the beat or rhythm being studied to the class while it is sitting on the floor.

2.   Limit the first expressions of the rhythmic pattern to hand clapping, foot stamping, head nodding or some other isolated movement.

3.   When the rhythm has been faily well established, while it is seated on the floor have the class move **many body parts** to the rhythm.

4.   Next, **stand** and isolate the expression of the rhythm to one action —again—foot stamping, striking with the arm, etc.

5.   Progress further by having the class express the rhythm in place but by moving many body parts either in unison or in sequence.

6.   Again isolate the action to one body part but perform this while moving from one place to another; e.g. walk while changing the position of the arms to the rhythm.

7.   Allow total body movement in rhythms while moving from one place to another.

8.   Apply the rhythmic pattern to a creative presentation:

   a.   . . . as individuals moving en masse to individualized presentations.

   b.   . . . in small groups with each participant creating his own pattern but with the group presenting its individual patterns simultaneously.

   c.   . . . in a group following a rhythmic pattern developed by a member of the group.

d.   . . . in a group and in unison—first performing the pattern developed by one of the group members and then progressing through the rhythmic patterns created by each other group member.

Depending on the age level, general ability, and previous experience of the class, this suggested sequence may take place in one rhythmic unit. More likely, however, progressions 8b through 8d will occur in the class' third or fourth year of rhythms.

Ideas

I.   Using one to four different colored pieces of construction paper, develop rhythmic patterns to the "rhythmic sounds" of the papers' colors.

   3/4 A.   RED RED RED/ RED RED RED/ RED RED RED/ RED RED RED

   4/4 B.   RED RED RED RED/ RED RED RED RED/ RED RED RED RED/ RED RED RED RED
Stress accents
RÉD RED RED RED/ RÉD RED RED RED/ etc.

       C.   YÉLLOW YÉLLOW YÉLLOW YÉLLOW/ YÉLLOW YÉLLOW YÉLLOW YÉLLOW/ etc.

For syncopation, experimenting with a change of accent

YÉLLOW YELLOW YÉLLOW YÉLLOW/ YÉLLOW YELLOW YÉLLOW YÉLLOW

YELLOW YÉLLOW YÉLLOW YELLOW/ YELLOW YÉLLOW YÉLLOW YELLOW

       D.   Combine colors

         1. RED RED YELLOW YELLOW

         2. RED YELLOW YELLOW RED

         3. YELLOW YELLOW YELLOW RED

         4. etc.

       E.   Add new colors. Stress the likeness of some "rhythmic sound".

         1. Red, blue, green, black, brown all have the same "rhythmic sound".

         2. Yellow, orange, purple also share "rhythmic sound".

       F.   Make up rhythmic patterns using a variety of colors.

         1. RED YELLOW GREEN BLUE/ RED YELLOW GREEN BLUE

      2. GREEN BLUE YELLOW RED/
         GREEN BLUE YELLOW RED

      3. BLUE GREEN RED YELLOW/
         BLUE GREEN RED YELLOW

  G. Divide the class into groups and assign each group an order of colors. Possibly a single color can be the common accent sound for all groups. Have the groups develop movement patterns to these orders of colors. Each group can present its creation and then if desirable the class can perform each other's patterns.

II. Follow the basic progression for IDEA 1, but use names of children in the class.

  A. JANE JANE JANE JANE/ JANE JANE JANE JANE

  B. BOBBY BOBBY BOBBY BOBBY/ BOBBY BOBBY BOBBY BOBBY

  C. DOROTHY DOROTHY DOROTHY DOROTHY DOROTHY DOROTHY DOROTHY DOROTHY

  D. Group the children according to like "rhythmic sounds".

    1. All Janes, Gails, Bruces, Karls in one group.

    2. Johnny, Carol, Stephen and Kathy in another group.

    3. Timothy, Dorothy, Caroline, Marguerite making up the third group.

    4. Children with unique name sounds without partners in the class can be grouped together for a very effective creation based on each of their name sounds.

III. Develop the learning of musical phrases through the use of partners or by dividing the class into two large groups (possible boys/girls). A good analogy in the concept of musical phrases is the idea of questions and answers. One phrase asks the question while the following phrase answers the question. To an established beat (or rhythm if the class is more advanced) have the first partner or group create a "question" through movement. The second group can either imitate the movement for the answer or it can create its own answers.

  A. Example:

Question	Mary	WALK WALK WALK WALK
Answer	Bobby	RUN-RUN RUN-RUN RUN-RUN RUN-RUN

or

| Question | Mary | SWING SWING SWING SWING |
| Answer | Bobby | WALK WALK JUMP LAND |

This same analogy between musical terms and grammatical terms can be expanded to include musical measures.

IV.   Since movement is the most fundamental form of communication, it is fun to study the history of the development of communication through rhythms. The teacher can expand upon this concept by including her own creative ideas. On the following page are just a few thoughts:

A. Because movement at the "personal confrontation" level was the first means of communication, the class can be encouraged to communicate emotions, anxieties, needs, threats, etc. to a "listener" or receiver who answers through movement. A concerted effort should be made for a MESSAGE TO BE TRANSMITTED through these actions. It may be desirable initially for the class to decide on the idea they wish to communicate; for example, the danger of a forest fire. Later each sender of the message can create his own idea for the receiver to comprehend and answer in a meaningful manner. A discussion of man's first attempt at communication can be discussed here. The need for language undoubtedly will be felt by the class.

B. Exclamatory words can next be enacted—the kinds of words first uttered by man. Following this, onomatopoeic expressions and words can be explored. Examples of the two above suggestions are:

1. "OH" "WHEW" "OUCH" "YIPES"
The children interpret the feelings of these words through movement.

2. "CRASH" "THUNDER" "BUZZ" "SWISH"
In conjunction with this, man's first attempts at verbal communication can be studied.

C. The next logical step would be to explore some of the media of mass communication in an historical progression.

The drum is the first primitive device to be considered. Moving to different rhythmical patterns created on the drum provides limitless movement problems. The class can devise drum beats which communicate to them the essence of messages sent through this medium.

1. Rapid, frenzied beats representing danger.
   Slow "mono-rhythmic" beats of death.
   Quick light, optimistic beats conveying a happy occurrence — possibly the first rain of a season.

D. Finally the Morse Code may be explored. Because of the nature of the quick, sharp clicks of the Morse Code a natural movement study could center around striking or ballistic actions. The class could learn correct Morse Code messages and develop movements around these.

PROGRAMS FOR CONFINED AREAS

Much of movement exploration can be taught in rather confined areas such as may be experienced during inclement weather, short breaks in the classroom routine, or when space is generally limited by facilities.

Examples of types of exploratory activities that are possible during the above times are: axial motions, balancing activities, stretches, contractions, walking, hopping, some jumping, collapsing and combinations of two or more of these activities. In addition, the concepts of levels, direction, space awareness, force and flow can be explored as separate entities or in combination with each other by use of the activities suggested for confined areas. The emphasis of lessons involving the above activities or concepts can be in the area of rhythms, stunts and tumbling or general skill development.

If a class is only temporarily confined to a limited area during lessons in movement exploration, it is suggested that the units being studied merely be continued indoors with emphasis on that part of the unit that can be conducted in a relatively small area. For example, the stunts and tumbling program which can be most dynamic out doors can be conducted temporarily inside where students could concentrate on improving balance, increasing flexibility and improving in other aspects of skill that are basic to high performance in stunts and tumbling.

If, however, it is expected that a class will be confined to a small area over a period of several weeks, a unit in rhythms can be planned for that time. Of all the facets of physical education, at the elementary school level, rhythms are most adaptable to the classroom or multipurpose room.

The following section contains sample questions and three sets of lesson plans. They are the suggested progressive steps in building a program in Movement Exploration. Depending on the age level of the class, it may be necessary to modify the phrasing of the question.

Chapter IV
Sample Lesson Plans

The daily, weekly, and yearly plans presented in this section should in no way limit the creativity of the reader's program but should serve merely as guides.

(Fourth Grade — First Week)

MONDAY

1. Boys and girls, what do you do when the whistle blows?
   (stop, look and listen)

2. Now, to be sure you understand that, in a minute you will run in a big circle going this (gesture) way. Stop, look and listen when the whistle blows.

3. (Repeat three or four times.)

4. Now, boys and girls, turn around this (gesture) way and let's see if you can stop to the whistle just as well going this direction.

5. (Repeat two or three times.)

6. How high into the air can you go?

7. Can you go higher?

8. What can you do to jump high but softly? (Recognize someone who has his hand raised to answer.)

9. Boys and girls, each of you bend your knees and land on the balls of your feet this time. Go.

10. Freeze. Now turn and face the person closest to you. That is your partner. If you don't have a partner, raise your hand. Go to that partner.

11. One partner curl up on the ground very tightly. Can the other partner go over him? Take turns.

12. Who can make a bridge, leaving room for water to run underneath?

13. Can you make a long, low bridge? A high, short bridge? Repeat several times.

14. How else can you make a bridge.

15. Can you make a bridge using one hand and two feet?

16.   Now can you make a bridge using one hand and one foot and hold for the count of seven?

17.   Who can hop in place? When one foot tires, practice on the other foot.

18.   Can you hop backward? . . . forward? . . . in a circle?

19.   Can you hop as quietly as you jumped?

20.   Show me a balancing position. Remember that when you balance your base should remain steady and still.

21.   How else can you balance?

22.   In how many different ways can you balance on a two point base?

23.   Balancing on one foot, how far can you lean forward, sideways and backward without falling? Try that on the other foot.

24.   Who can balance on his seat?

25.   How long can you balance with just your hands on the ground? Count the amount of time you are in that position. Can you improve your time? How many improved?

26.   Can you balance on one knee? On two? Which is easier?

27.   Show me how you can roll.

28.   Who can roll like a log? Roll back again. Watch out for others who are rolling.

29.   Now can you roll like a ball?

30.   Who can roll like a wheel?

31.   What else rolls? Can you roll like it? Can you come back again?

Evaluation — Some Possible Questions Relating to This Lesson

1.   How do you land softly from a jump or hop?

2.   What is the difference between a jump and hop?

3.   What makes balancing easy or difficult?

4.   What is the simplest balancing position? What is a difficult balancing position for you?

TUESDAY

1.   Run as quickly as you can in that (gesture) direction until the whistle blows.

2.   Run back until the whistle blows.

3.   Run as fast as you can and then on the word, "jump," jump as far as you can.

4. Try it again seeing if you can jump farther this time.

5. How high can you jump?

6. Freeze and look at the person next to you. Go to that partner.

7. Can you leap or jump over your partner? Take turns.

8. How high can your partner be when you jump or leap over him without touching?

9. Can you leap or jump higher?

10. In what way could you use your arms to help you jump higher?

11. Show me a longer, lower bridge than yesterday's.

12. Can you make a very different shaped bridge?

13. Can you and your partner make a bridge together?

14. Make a long low bridge.

15. How could this be a drawbridge?

16. Can one partner crawl under the bridge and then go over it without touching?

17. How low a bridge can you go under and how high can the bridge you jump over be? Be careful of bumping. Take turns.

18. How long can you keep just your hands on the ground?

19. See if you can do it longer each time.

20. Can you move your hands in a walking motion while in this position?

21. Who can stretch very high while in this position?

22. Let's skip forward quickly.

23. How high off the ground can you lift on every skip?

24. Can you let your arms help you gain height? How? Show me.

25. Can you skip backward?

26. Find your old partner. Can you skip together?

27. In how many ways can you skip together?

28. Try skipping while facing each other.

Evaluation

1. How do leaping and jumping differ from one another?

2. Is it easier to jump or leap for height?

3. How many people were able to balance on their hands longer today than yesterday? What made it easier today?

WEDNESDAY

1. Can you do a stunt while jumping? Show me.

2. Who can turn around while jumping? How far can you turn?

3. Can you turn as far in the opposite direction while jumping?

4. How high can your partner hold his arm and have you clear it by jumping? Trade positions.

5. Can you jump higher by doing a standing jump or a running jump? Practice to find out.

6. Let's see who can balance on his hands even longer today than yesterday.

7. Can you walk in that position?

8. If you can hold the handstand position, can you do a split?

9. How much space can you fill with your body?

10. Make yourself as wide as possible.

11. Can you change positions, still taking up a great deal of space?

12. How long can you be?

13. In what other way could you be long and thin?

14. How small can you make yourself?

15. Can you become even smaller?

16. Now find a very crooked position.

17. Be crooked in another way.

18. Try this time to bend or twist every possible joint.

19. Can you move while in a very crooked position?

20. Quickly run to the circle (on the blacktop).

21. Who can move around the circle in any direction without bumping a classmate? Show me.

22. Can you do this while moving faster?

23. Can you skip in this area without colliding?

24. Skip back to the grass until the whistle blows.

25. How can you move in that (gesture) direction, moving just your arms? Find a way and show me.

26. Can you come back to your home space that way?

27. Can you move in that direction (gesture) using your hands and feet?

28. Can you come back the same way except feet first?

29. How else can you move with your hands and feet on the ground? Can you find another different way?

30. Who can balance on a three point base?

31. What other way can you balance on a three point base?

32. Using something other than both feet, can you balance on a two point base?

33. Can you balance in a high position?

34. Can you balance in a low position?

35. Practice some of the rolls you tried yesterday.

36. Can you roll forward and backward?

37. With your arms around your legs, can you roll in a complete circle?

Evaluation

1. Is it easier to balance in a high or low position? Why?

2. Is it easier to balance in a two or three point base? Why?

3. What activities today took a great deal of strength?

4. When you were moving about in the circle on the blacktop, how did you avoid bumping?

5. Do you have more control moving slowly or quickly?

THURSDAY

1. Notice where you are standing. That is home base. On the signal, "go", move anywhere you wish; but when I call, "home base," return home as quickly as possible without bumping. "Go." (Repeat several times.)

2. Change your home base and let's try that again. Can you do it this time without looking at home base while you are moving? (Repeat several times.)

3. Can you run forward?

4. Now try to run backward.

5. Look at the person closest to you. That is your partner. Go to him.

6. Face each other. One be the leader. Run in many different directions, seeing if your partner can stay facing you and with you without bumping. Take turns as the leader.

7. Work some more on your hand stands. Try to beat your record for staying up.

8. Who can keep his arms around his lower legs and roll back and forth until he is standing up?

9. Try this many times.

10. With your partner make bridges and leap over. We will have a quick contest to see who can clear the highest bridge without bumping. I will select the couple to demonstrate.

11. How high can your partner hold his hand for you to successfully clear? Take turns leaping.

12. Facing that (gesture) way, on "go", run quickly and leap as far as you possibly can.

13. Try it again to see if you can leap further.

14. You and your partner take turns.

FRIDAY

1. Find a different way to move from here to the edge of the grass and back.

2. Who can go to the edge of the grass in a way he has never tried before?

3. Come back to home base using your hands and feet.

4. Can you go that direction (gesture) moving feet first?

5. Find a partner. One partner be the base and one the top. In what position can you be so that the top man does not touch the ground?

6. Can you find another way to be so that the top man does not touch the ground?

7. Join up with the couple nearest to you. What can the four of you do in the form of a pyramid? (Discuss safety of foot placement, etc.)

8. Can you build a different pyramid?

9. Can you have two bases and two top men?

10. What can you do with three bases and one top man?

11. Stunt relays.

12. Tug - o - war.

WEEKLY LESSON PLAN NO. 1

MONDAY

1. Review directions – stop, look and listen
2. Jumping (height, distance, over partner)
3. Make bridges – several combinations – high, low
4. Hopping – in place – forward, backward, in a circle
5. Balancing – one part of body – two parts, etc. – twisting
6. Rolling – like wheel – log – ball

TUESDAY

1. Running – jumping – leaping
2. Bridges – high – low – creative – partners
3. Crawling – under bridges
4. Hand stand – just get feet off ground
5. Leaping – over bridges – over partner – distance – height
6. Skipping – forward – backward – partner – around obstacle

WEDNESDAY

1. Jumping – over object for height – distance – partner
2. Hand stand – try for longer period of time
3. Space – make yourself large, small, crooked, with partner, long
4. Run – stop – start – change directions
5. Stunts – seal walk – crab walk – elephant walk
6. Balance – one part of body – more than one
7. Rolling – log – ball – wheel

THURSDAY

1. Space – move to new space – front – back – sides
2. Running – with partner – different speeds – jumping
3. Hand stand
4. Roll – back and forth – get up on feet
5. Bridge – with partner – without partner – creative
6. Leap – height – distance

FRIDAY

1. Stunts – crab – seal – simple pyramid – somersaults
2. Relays – learned skills
3. Tug - o - war – partners – teams

WEEKLY LESSON PLAN NO. 2

MONDAY

1. Balls – directions to get ball – where to bounce
2. Bouncing – high – low – turn – change hands – different part of body
3. Throwing – toss up catch – toss higher, clap and a catch – clap many times and catch (count) – for distance – accuracy
4. Striking – with fist many times
5. Volleying – to partner – to self – against wall – against backboard
6. Rolling – run and catch at a certain point
7. Jumping – over ball – catching ball while in the air

TUESDAY

1. Bounce – moving – standing still – turning – alternate hands – moving in and around obstacles – high – low – sitting down – ball around you – ball half way around
2. Rolling – run and meet – jump over – circle around
3. Feet – get ball from feet to hands – take ball overhead with just feet – hold ball six inches off ground
4. Volleying – keep ball overhead

WEDNESDAY

1. Bounce – running – walking – turning – sitting – leg over ball (alternate)

2. Throwing – toss and catch – distance – hard to ground jump and catch

3. Feet – ball from feet to hands – hold over head – off ground 6 inches – dribble – jump over

4. Tossing – bounce ball high, catch low – let ball bounce – turn around and catch it

5. Balance – ball on back of hand – palm – finger – head – shoulder

6. Strike – ball with fist – keep in air

THURSDAY

1. Bounce – repeat above

2. Work with partners – rolls – volleys – pass ball with feet

3. Passes – to partner – underhand – overhand – bounce

4. Holding ball – take around yourself without touching – different ways to take ball around yourself – hold ball in front of you with both hands – take hands away quickly, return and catch ball before it falls

5. Holding – place ball behind head – take hands away – catch without turning around

6. Repeat above activities with partners

FRIDAY

1. Relays – ball handling

2. Dodge ball variations with more than one ball

3. Throw for distance

WEEKLY LESSON PLAN NO. 3

MONDAY

1. Bounce – low – high – moving – ball around self – part way around – from knee to hand – ball hard to ground jump and catch – jump, catch and turn – other part of body

2. Rolling – run and catch – roll to partner – let ball run up to leg – to hands

3. Volley – head to partner – hands to partner – knee to partner

4. Kicking – rolling ball – stationary – punt

5. Tossing – high clap and catch – high clap many times and catch – high turn and catch – catch low

6. Feet – dribble – return ball to hands

TUESDAY

1. Bounce – to partner – run bounce to partner
2. Volley – with partner –(review)
3. Feet – to partner's hands – dribble – pass to partner
4. Partner – back to back ball around each other – find other ways to get ball around – join with a group – find many ways to pass balls to each other.
5. Partner – side arm throw – overhand throw

WEDNESDAY

1. Running – circle – around field – stop and start – change directions
2. Challenge – hop to distant point – skip to another – jump – return running
3. Tires – run around – foot in – feet in – jump on both sides
4. Blocks – obstacle course
5. Space – run – freeze – collapse
6. Jump – astride – scissors – high (give these quickly)

THURSDAY

1. Gallop – alone – with partner
2. Skip – forward – backward – with partner
3. Balance – on each foot – eyes closed
4. Space – with balls – walk, slow bounce – faster bounce
5. Hurdle – several low hurdles
6. Benches – run over top – crawl under – run lengthwise – find other ways – vault over one – vault over two benches stacked together (benches should be held by students to prevent tipping)

FRIDAY

1. Obstacle-course for agility
2. Hurdles – time
3. Relays – through stationary obstacle

WEEKLY LESSON PLAN NO. 4

Divide class into three groups. Stagger instructions so the first group is ready for instruction when the third group has just begun its activity.

MONDAY
(Apparatus — Balance Beam)

1. Safety – turns – names of apparatus

2. Horizontal – parazontal – ladders – single outside rail – double rail – single rung – double rung – pass in middle – hang by hands – hang by any two limbs – different limbs – cross in a different way – go in and out of rungs

3. Rings – forward travel – hold two rings – swing legs – hang 30 seconds

4. Horizontal bar – climb to highest bar – chin yourself – hang by hands and feet – hang by one leg, one hand

TUESDAY

1. Repeat – be certain each group works at each piece of equipment

WEDNESDAY

1. Apparatus – use all pieces of equipment as an obstacle course

2. Balance Beam – low board or boundary rail – low fence – heel toe across forward – heel toe backward – stop in middle bounce

3. Balance – turn – go low – first balance on one foot and then the other

THURSDAY

1. Apparatus – hang – drop (land lightly, bend knees) – climb over the top – travel backward – single rail – double rail – chin self – cross with two hands, two legs – think of new methods

2. Rotate groups through horizontal ladder – parazontal ladder – horizontal bar – balance beam

3. Groups that finish explore jungle gym – or work on stairs

4. Picnic tables – vault on – run across jump off – low bench – table top – find different ways of getting on and off – try a new way

FRIDAY

1. Climbing – tether ball poles – ropes

2. Steal the flag

3. End ball

4. Folk and square dancing

	WEEK I	WEEK II	WEEK III	WEEK IV
SEPT	Establishing discipline procedures. Running, starting, stopping, stretching, jumping, bridges, hopping, rolling, spatial awareness.	Running, bridges, jumping, rolling, balancing, turning, twisting, combination of skills learned, changing of directions.	Running, stretching, bridges, balancing, jumping, twisting, turning, shaking, walking board or balance beam.	Running, crawling, walking, jumping, bridges, turning, twisting, rolling, walking board, obstacle course.
OCT	Running, bridges, crawling under partner's bridge, jumping, rolling, ball bouncing to self, ball bouncing to partner, walking board, obstacle course, flash cards.	Running with partner, bridges with partner, see-saw with partner, rolling, jumping, ball bouncing, change level while bouncing. Game (6:401)*	Ball bouncing self, partner, bouncing at different levels, walk while bouncing, turn while bouncing, tossing ball to self, space awareness with balls.	Bouncing at different levels, bouncing while walking, different directions, bouncing while turning, tossing to self, tossing to partner.
NOV	Rolling ball to partner. Tossing ball to self, toss, bounce, catch. bounce, turn, catch. Game (5:64)	Toss, bounce, catch. Bounce turn, catch. Toss, clap, catch. Roll to partner. Bouncing while moving faster. Game (5:65) Choice Day (1:183) (1:184)	Bounce pass to partner. Balance while bouncing. Bounce while moving faster. Kick ball to partner. Kick, run, kick again. Bounce through obstacle course. (1:183) (1:184)	Bounce pass to partner. Kick to partner. Kick, run, kick again. Strike ball with fist and retrieve. Game (5:65) Modify for kicking obstacle course.
DEC	Running, jumping, ball bouncing to self. Bounce obstacle course, kicking obstacle course.	Roll ball under partner's bridge. Run and jump. Donkey kick. Sit and pick up ball with feet. Hold ball with feet high above head. Toss ball through hoop. Choice day.		
JAN	Rhythms using sounds of colors (e.g. red, red, red) or (yellow, yellow, yellow) Rhythms using names (e.g. Timmy, Timmy, Timmy)	Rhythms using months (e.g. January) Rhythms using sentences (e.g. I am happy)	Rhythms using animal e.g. Whinny Moo Meow Woof Quack, quack Flash cards	Rhythms using above ideas Work in groups of 3 or 4 Present to rest of class Indian theme dance presentation

FEB Climbing, picnic table, benches, jumping off. Jumping off benches over baton. Climbing over picnic table. Obstacle course stressing right from left.	Climbing benches, jumping off. Climbing over picnic table. Low horizontal bar. Horizontal ladder. Walking up and down stairs.	Low horizontal bar. Horizontal ladder. Rolling, galloping, hopping, leaping. Locomotor skills along benches. Stairs	Galloping, leaping, leaping over lying partner, horizontal ladder, rolling, jumping off bench, landing, rolling. Ladder. Choice Day.
MAR Galloping, rolling. Ladder, only hands on stairs. Ground	Jump over stretched jump rope. Crawl under rope, roll over rope, leap over rope. Jump rope swinging back and forth. Jump low hurdles. (3:69-76)	Roll hula hoop to partner, climb through hula hoop held by partner, push hula hoop and chase it, roll through hula hoop held by partner. Low hurdles.	Roll hula hoop to partner. Jump into hula hoop held by partner. Push hula hoop, run and crawl through it. Make hula hoop roll back to self. Leap into hula hoop held by partner.
APR Go through hula hoop held by partner. Roll hula hoop; run and crawl through it. Make hoop roll back to self. Make hoop spin. Run and roll hoop. Choice Day	Throw ball through hoop held by partner. Bounce ball through hoop held by partner. Toss ball through hoop held like a basket by partner. Make hoop spin. Batons.	Ball tossing to self. Ball throwing to partner. Kick ball to partner. Bounce ball while making a bridge. Roll over ball. Hold ball between feet while sitting. Batons, ball and hoops.	Bounce ball with another part of body, i.e., elbow. Roll ball, run and get it. Bounce ball at different levels. Leap over ball. Roll over ball. Game (6:372)
MAY Stand on hands. Jump over partner who is making a low bridge. Running at different levels. Swinging. Bridges. Game (6:363)	Horizontal ladder—traveling, hanging, crossing, swinging. Horizontal bar—chinning, hanging, climb bar. Climb on table and jump off. Obstacle Course Choice Day	Horizontal ladder—traveling, hanging, crossing, swinging. Climb on table and jump off. Cross table in a new way. Jump off table, land, roll.	
JUNE Balance bean bag on foot and hop. Balance bean bag on different place and move. Bean bag toss for accuracy. Favorite Games	Walk on hands and feet. Balance on hands. Roll. Jump and roll. Jump and leap. Run and jump. Choice Week	*Numbers indicate book and page in suggested reading list.	

	WEEK I	WEEK II	WEEK III	WEEK IV
S E P T	Establishing discipline procedure. Running. Starting. Stopping. Bridges. Rolling. Hopping. Stretching. Space awareness. Tire and block obstacle course.	Running. Rolling. Bridges. Walking different levels. Walking different directions. Jumping. Walking on hands and feet. Tire and block obstacle course. Game (6:363)	Running different levels. Walking hands and feet. Jumping different directions. Rolling. Hopping. Walking different levels and directions. Putting hands only on ground.	Running. Donkey kick. Walking different levels and directions. Walking different speeds. Rolling. Bridges. Hopping. Twisting. Balancing.
O C T	Running. Balancing. Turning. Twisting. Walking and twisting. Combination of skills learned. Bridges. Galloping. Donkey kick. Balance board. Flash cards. Game (6:372)	Running different levels and directions. Turning. Balancing. Leaping. Bridges. Crawling. Combination of skills learned. Balance board. Walking board.	Walking different levels with partner. Running with partner. Bridges and crawling with partner. Leaping over partner. Ladder—oblique. Choice Day.	Running different directions with partner. Bridges and crawling with partner. Balancing with partner. Leaping over partner. Jumping over partner. Ladder. Walking board.
N O V	Ball bouncing. Ball bouncing at different levels. Ball bouncing while moving. Hold ball over head with feet. Toss ball with feet. Roll over ball. Space awareness with balls.	Ball bouncing while moving. Ball bouncing at different levels. Ball tossing. Ball tossing to partner. Bounce, pass to partner. Roll over ball. Jump over stationary ball. Ball tricks. e.g. drop, turn and catch. Create own games.	Running. Moving faster while bouncing ball. Passing ball to partner feet to feet. Bouncing at different levels. Ball tossing to partner. Throwing for distance and chase. Game (5:81) (5:66)	Moving faster while bouncing ball. Bounce ball while moving in different directions. Pass ball to partner feet to feet. Roll over ball. Jump over ball. Throw through hoop. Choice Day
D E C	Jump over all. Donkey kick over ball. Ball tossing to partner. Ball passing feet to feet. Ball bouncing different levels. Ball rolling to partner. Throw through swinging hoop. Dribble with feet.	Toss, bounce, pass. Bounce, turn, catch. Other combinations. Roll to partner. Toss ball with feet. Roll ball under partner's bridge. Each partner with ball toss to each other. Choice Day	Pass ball to partner while moving. Strike ball with different part of body to partner. Use feet in doing something new with the ball. Balance with the ball. Balance the ball.	Free play with balls.
J A N	Move from one place to another using the ball in some way. Another way. Do something to make the ball go high and low. Explore other space problems with ball. Do something new with ball. Strike ball with fist. Game—ball relays	Kick ball, run after it, kick again. Run while bouncing ball. Bounce with different part of body. Balance ball in some way. Roll with ball. Strike ball to partner with different part of body. Dribble with feet.		

FEB	Rhythms using colors (red, red, red, red). (Red, yellow, red, yellow) Rhythms using names (John, John, John) Walking in different directions and at different levels. Stress accents (Johnny)	Rhythms using names (Johnny, Johnny) Running different ways. Rhythms using animal sounds (peep, peep) (moo, moo) (ba, ba) Stress accents.	Rhythms using names (Johnathan, Johnathan) Quick running steps in different directions and levels. Questions and answers. (One group ask questions on red; other respond on yellow.)	Creative group work. Divide by name sounds (e.g., Mary and Tommy in same group). Group present project to rest of class. Draw movement patterns.
MAR	Stairs. Running and jumping. Climbing picnic table, bench, crossing, jumping off. High jump. Long jump.	Climbing onto table, cross, jump off. Get on table a different way, cross, jump off. Get on table, cross in a different way. Jump off. Stairs. Choice Day	Get on table. Cross in a different way. Get off in a different way. Low horizontal bar. Horizontal ladder. Stilts.	Low horizontal bar. Horizontal ladder. Crossing, hanging, swinging. Try many different ways. Hurdles.
APR	Low horizontal bar. Horizontal ladder. Using just arms. Using 1 arm and 2 legs. Hanging new ways. Hurdles. Obstacle course. Choice Day	Jump over stretched rope. Leap over stretched rope. Hop over rope. Roll over rope. Crawl under rope. Go under then back over rope. Stilts. Balance Board. (3:69-76)	Jump, leap, hop over higher rope. Go over a new way. Go over rope swinging back and forth. Jump over rope, land, roll. (3:69-76) Create own games.	Jump over higher rope. Go over higher rope swinging back and forth. Experiment by self with hula hoop. Send hula hoop to partner. Spin hoop.
MAY	Send hoop to partner. Spin hoop. Roll hoop, run, go through hoop. Hop in and out of hoop which is lying on ground. Pick up hoop with feet. Relays with hoops.	Roll hoop, run, catch it. Roll hoop back to self. Throw ball through hoop held by partner. Toss ball through hoop held as basket. Jump into hoop held by partner. Throw ball through swinging hoop.	Roll hoop, run, catch it. Jump through hoop held by partner. Roll through hoop held by partner. Hold hoop in hands and twist in many directions and levels.	Pick up hoop with feet. Roll through hoop held by partner. Twist with hoop. Roll hoop, run, go through it. Twirl hoop with some part of body. Choice Day. Stairs. Create own games.
JUNE	Twirl hoop with some part of body. Using all equipment and apparatus of the year have free play. Rotate groups.	Free play with all equipment and apparatus.		

	WEEK I	WEEK II	WEEK III	WEEK IV
SEPT	Establishing discipline procedure. Running, stretching, jumping, bridges, galloping, rolling, hopping, Space awareness. Flash cards. Word patterns.	Running. Bridges with partner crawling underneath. Hopping in different directions. Stretching. Running and jumping. Other combinations of skills. Game (6:364) Word Patterns	Running with partner. Bridges—partners crawl under, then jump over. Walking at different levels. Rolling, balancing. Twisting. Tire and block obstacle course Game (6:371)	Running with partner at different levels. Bridges—partner going over and under. Turning. Running and jumping. Walking on hands and feet. Stairs.
OCT	Using different locomotor skills. Running, walking, different levels. Rolling. Seal walk. Sliding. Only hand on ground. Balancing on different parts of body.	Seal walk. Sliding. Walking different levels and directions. Rolling. Bridges—partner over and under. Stairs. Ladder. Game (6:405)	Stairs, Ladder. Seal walk. Running. Rolling. Leaping. Donkey kick. Sliding. Wheels. Galloping. Walking different speeds. Turning. Twisting. Choice Day. Game (6:407) Stilts	Twisting, turning. Moving different speeds. Seal walk. Running and jumping. Leaping over partner. Donkey kick. Wheels. Stilts. Game (6:409)
NOV	Ball bouncing to self. Moving while bouncing. Bouncing at different levels. Donkey kick over the ball. Sitting, pick up ball with feet. Get ball from feet to hands. Kicking with feet. Game (5:83) (5:73)	Ball bouncing while moving. Tossing to self. Bounce at different levels. Donkey kick over the ball. Leap over the ball. Sit and pick up ball with feet. Hand and foot dribbles through obstacle courses.	Throwing. Bouncing different levels and directions. Tossing to self. Donkey kick over ball. Leap over ball. Pick ball up with feet and get it to hands. Volleying to self. Game (5:73) (5:70) (1:184)	Ball tossing to partner. Bounce toss to partner. Sit pass ball feet to feet with partner. Kick to partner. Leap over ball. Toss, bounce, and catch. Volleying to partner. Create own games.
DEC	Bounce while moving quickly. Tossing high and catching. Bounce, passing to partner. Overhand throw to partner. Kicking to partner. Tossing ball with feet to partner. Two-square.	Choice Day Ball practice around obstacles; two square, bouncing up and down stairs. Create own games		
JAN	Bridges—partner roll ball under bridge. Roll over ball. Kick, run, kick again. Punting.	Leap on picnic table bench, run, jump off. Repeat for distance. Ladder, balance board, balance beam. Choice Day	Leap on bench, run, get off different way. Leap on bench, jump off, land, roll. Leap on bench, cross a different way, get off a different way, balance board, balance beam	Leap on, cross, get off a different way. Leap on, lie down and get off. Climb onto table, cross jump off. Repeat for height. Repeat for distance.

F E B	Get on table, cross in a different way. Get on table a different way, cross, get off backward. Cross horizontal ladder with hands only. Table Relays	Repeat table activities. Cross horizontal ladder using hands and legs. Cross in a different way, hang by hands and legs. Cross one way, hang by hands and drop to ground. Hang using only 2 limbs. Hang using 2 different limbs. Obstacle Course	Go across the top of the ladder. Go the length of the ladder backward. Weave in and out of ladder. Cross one side of ladder. Hurdles, timing on hurdles.	Timing on hurdles. Stilts. Choice Day Stairs.
M A R	Rhythms: Using sounds of colors in Spanish. (Rojo, Rojo, Rojo) (Amarillo, Amarillo, Amarillo). Using Spanish words for months. Work on accents and phrases.	Rhythms: Questions and answers. One group moves (question)—second group moves (answer), i.e., (How are you?) (We are fine.) Drawing, movement patterns, moving to moods.	Rhythms—specific rhythms assigned to all. Break into groups of 3 or 4. Each compose own movements to be presented to the class. Simple folk dances.	Crawl under stretched jump rope. Jump over stretched rope. Jump rope, long rope. (3:69-74)
A P R	Jump over rope. Roll over rope, swinging back and forth.	Individual ropes. Jump rope. Step on one end and pull in different directions against resistance. With partner; one remains stationary, other moves against resistance. Jump rope, long rope.	Roll hoop to partner. Roll hoop, run and go through. Spin hoop. Roll, run, roll again. Roll hoop bact to self. Jump long rope. Hop scotch.	Roll hoop, run, and go through hoop. Roll back to self. Roll, run to hoop, roll again. Spin hoop on some part of body. Choice Day
M A Y	Roll through hoop held by partner. Toss ball through hoop. Toss ball through hoop held like a basket. Jump into hoop held by partner.	Hoop on ground, jump into and out of. Pick up hoop with feet. Roll hoop, run to it, roll it again. Spin hoop with different part of body. Hoop Relays	Hold hoop in 2 hands, twist and bend in many directions. Toss hoop up and catch it. Jump into hoop held by partner. Go through hoop held by partner. Create own games.	Hula hoop relay. Ball relay using skills of the past units. Ball Games (5:248) (5:248) (5:265)
J U N E	Different hula hoop relays. Different ball relays. Obstacle Course Tug-O-War Four-Square	Free week using all equipment of the year. Ball Games (5:278) Repeat Others		

	WEEK I	WEEK II	WEEK III	WEEK IV
SEPT	Establishing discipline procedure. Starting, running, stopping. Rolling. Bridges. Running and leaping combination. Only hands on ground, space awareness. Game (6:409)	Running. Bridges. Rolling. Running and leaping partner in bridge position. Rolling over partner in bridge position. Jumping. Obstacle course Game (6:405)	Running. Leaping and jumping over partner's bridge. Rolling. Jumping. Skipping. Rolls, Stairs. Balance Board. Walking Board.	Game using learned skills. Leaping or jumping over partner. Skipping. Hand balancing. Choice Day Walking Board.
OCT	Game with social interaction. Hand balancing. Skipping. Jumping. Fast running. Hurdles. Balance Board. Walking Board. Game (6:402)	Relays involving locomotor skills. Skipping. Hand balancing. Rolling over partner. Stilts, walking board, stairs.	Head stands. Long low bridges. Running with a partner. Running and rolling. Sliding. Stairs, ladder, stilts. Choice Day	Sliding with partner. Running with partner. Head stand. Wheels. Tug-O-War with partner. Stairs, ladder.
NOV	Balls. Bounce ball while at different levels. Do a stunt while bouncing the ball. Move quickly while bouncing ball. Bounce ball with different parts of body. Game (5:81)	Bounce ball while moving in different directions. Strike ball upward with the fist many times. Four square, throwing game (5:68) Create own games	Strike ball upward with a different part of the body. Bounce the ball hard; catch it as it comes back down. Repeat but jump to catch ball. Game (5:281) (5:283)	Repeat all of above. Roll the ball, run, get in front of it and catch it. Kick the ball and repeat. Pass the ball to partner.
DEC	Get the ball to partner in a different way. Do this another way. Jump with ball between feet. Sit down and pick ball up with feet. Choice Day Games (5:74) (1:185)	Sit facing partner, pass ball feet to feet. Toss ball to partner with feet to his hands. Try this a new way. Game (5:243)		
JAN	Horizontal ladder. Hanging with hands. Crossing using hands only. Crossing using hands and feet. Hanging by two limbs. Hanging a new way.	Repeat above, cross touching every other bar. Weave in and out of bars. Cross using one arm and two legs. Cross without using rungs.	Repeat above. Roll over swinging rope. Jump over long turning rope. While jumping long rope, try some stunt. Jump short rope. Hop rope, pepper.	Repeat above. Jump rope with individual rope. Move while jumping rope. Jump rope quickly. Jump to rhythms.

FEB	Groups of 3—try new ways of jumping over each other. Tug-of-war. Partner pushing. Skipping with partner. Hurdles Time on hurdles.	Tug-of-war. Wheels. Groups of 3—jumping. New active game. Running and leaping. Jumping for height or distance. Obstacle course. Time on hurdles.	Apparatus—picnic table. Leap onto table, run and jump off. Leap on, roll across, crawl off. Get on a new way. Roll across, crawl off, land and roll.	Repeat above. Get on table, wheel across, get off new way. Get on a new way. Slide across; get off a new way. Choice Day
MAR	Repeat all apparatus work. Leap or jump on table. Run across and clear a baton on the jump off. Jump off for height and/or distance. Stairs.	Get on and go across table. Jump off and roll. Go through sequence with completely new ideas. Relay using tables. Stairs.	Kick ball to partner. Kick ball, run and kick again many times. Toss ball against wall—jump over the rebound. Roll over ball. Jump over ball back and forth. Dribble with feet. Punt.	Pick ball up a new way. Do something new with ball while balancing. Toss ball and catch—toss as high as possible being able to catch ball. Foot dribble—obstacle course. Punt, drop kick.
APR	Ball relays. Volly ball in groups of 3. Volly ball over a stretched rope. Play simple team game using balls. Kick ball. Use other parts of body to volley.	Continue ball team game. New team game requiring different ball handling skills, i.e., simplified volley ball. Ball relays.	Obstacle course, i.e., ball bouncing, running, leaping, crossing, dismounting table. Rolling. Hand walking. Horizontal ladder. Continue game. Create own games.	Obstacle course. Continue team games.
MAY	Obstacle course. Hula hoops. Roll hoop, run and roll it again. Roll hoop ball to self. Toss hoop and catch. Roll through hoop held by partner.	Obstacle course. Roll hoop back to self and vault it. Roll hoop to partner. Roll hoop, partner dive through hoop. Jump in and out of hoop held by partner.	Obstacle course. Repeat hoop activities. Toss ball through hoop held by partner. Roll ball through moving hoop. Try something new with hoop and ball.	Obstacle course. Hula hoop relays. Ball and hoop relays. Games (5:251) (5:258)
JUNE	Obstacle course. Free play in groups—rotate daily from one area to another using all activities of the year. Games (5:260)	Obstacle course. Repeat preceding week's free play. Repeat games.	Note: Rhythmic movement exploration good rainy day lessons.	

	WEEK I	WEEK II	WEEK III	WEEK IV
SEPT	Establishing discipline procedure. Running, jumping, rolling, bridges, leaping, hopping, balancing. Jumping over bridges. Crawling under partner's bridge. Space Awareness.	Running. Running and jumping. Bridges. Leaping. Leaping over bridges. Crawling under bridges. Hand stands. Wheels. Skipping. Football skills—Forward Pass.	Running. Bridges. Running with partner. Moving in different speeds with partner. Ball bouncing. Bouncing ball at different levels. Bouncing ball with different body parts. Game (6:472)	Ball bouncing. Moving at different speeds while bouncing. Moving in different directions while bouncing. Bouncing with different body parts. Game (5:78)
OCT	Throwing ball to partner for distance. Throwing to partner, overhand and side arm. Kicking to partner. Punting to partner. Foot dribbling. Crack about.	Foot dribbling. Jumping over ball—forward, backward, sideways. Rolling over ball. Getting ball from feet to hands in a new way. Bouncing ball while moving. Game (5:73)	Bounce ball hard; jump and catch the ball as it comes down. Roll over ball. Pass ball to partner using feet only. Get ball from own feet to hands a new way. Game (6:470)	Throwing to partner for distance. Kicking to partner. Get ball to partner a different way. Jumping over ball. Game (5:69)
NOV	Roll ball, run, get in front of it. Dribble ball with feet. Kick ball to partner who stops it with feet. Bounce ball hard: jump to catch it. Game (5:75)	Volley ball with partner. Jump, keeping ball between feet. Sit; pick ball up with feet and pass to partner's feet. Do something different with ball. Game (5:232)	Relays with ball or no equipment. Game: Newcomb Game (5:240) (1:186) Create own games.	Game : Newcomb. Game—Modified volleyball. (1) Throw or regulation serve. (2) Any number or players hit the ball before it crosses the net. Game (5:277)
DEC	Apparatus: Picnic table. Leap on to table; run across and leap off. Repeat, leaping for distance. Leap on to table; run across and jump for distance. Repeat jumping for height. Tumbling. Simple rolls.	Repeat all of above. Get on table in a new way; cross in a new way and get off in a new way. Leap on to table; roll across and crawl off. Leap on, wheel across, get off in a new way. Tumbling—head stands	Horizontal ladder: Cross ladder using hands only. Cross ladder moving backward. Hang in a different way. Cross ladder using every other rung. Weave in and out of bars. Tumbling—rope climb.	Cross ladder using only side bar rail. Cross ladder using hands and feet. Do something different on ladder. Cross ladder using two feet and one hand. Tumbling. Pyramids.
JAN	Repeat all ladder activities. Free play using ladder and table. Divide into groups and rotate between apparatus. End ball. Game (6:470)	Relays using apparatus. Game: Dodge ball. Game: Bombardment (a form of dodge ball in which you can be hit unless you have the ball. May take only one	Game: Bombardment Game: Boundary Ball Any number of players. Ball thrown back and forth between teams. Object: Throw ball over opposing end line. May	Korobushka (5:291) Folk and square dancing. Game (5:165)

	Week 1	Week 2	Week 3	Week 4
FEB	Folk and square dancing. Korobushka (5:291) Dance (6:505) Game (5:158)	Folk and square dancing. Dance (6:503) Dance (5:291) Game (5:159)	Running for speed. Running and jumping as far as possible. Jumping over a stretched rope. Rolling over stretched rope. Instr (5:103) Game (5:160)	Obstacle course, e.g., horizontal bar. Run to picnic table, leap on, jump off and roll. Run around field once. Get ball and dribble with feet one lap. Pick ball up and walk back. Repeat preceding week. Game (5:160)
MAR	Jump ropes: Jumping with individual ropes. Hop roping; both feet. Jump roping in a small circle. Moving backward while jump roping. Jump for time—successive jumps.	Do something different with rope and jumping. Jump rope being turned with one hand as a lariat. With partner tug-of-war. Game: Jump the shot. Repeat preceding week. Basketball—free throw shooting. (3:69-76)	Ball handling: Striking ball with fist to partner. Striking ball with other body part to partner. Kicking ball to partner. Throwing to partner. Game: (5:165)	Game: Kickball—Coed. Hit pin soccer.
APR	Game: Kickball Same as preceding week.	Hula hoop: Rolling hoop, run, and roll again. Toss hoop and make it come back to self. Repeat, this time jumping hoop. Do something new with hoop. Newcomb Create own games.	Repeat above. Jump "rope" with hoop. Toss hoop and catch it. Roll hoop to partner. Repeat—partner jump hoop. Dive through hoop held by partner. Newcomb	Repeat above. Toss ball through hoop held by partner. Repeat from longer distance. Toss ball through hoop tossed up by partner. Toss ball through hoop rolled by partner. Instr (5:247)
MAY	Batons: Jump over baton held by partner. Dive over baton held by partner. Balance baton on hand. Balance baton a new way. Balance baton on ground; turn around and catch it. Game (5:247)	Repeat above. Sitting, hold baton at both ends and pass under lifted legs. Holding baton at both ends, step through it. Balance baton on foot. Walk sideways on wand. Game (5:249)	Balance baton on hand while moving as low as possible. Run while balancing baton. Do something new while balancing baton. Relays: Wands—Balls. Create own games.	Boys: Softball Girls: 2-square
JUNE	Free play rotating among all movement exploration units. Obstacle course. Balance beam. Folk square dance.	Free play rotating among all movement exploration units. Stunts—tumbling on mats.	Note: Rhythms using the movement exploration approach are good rainy day lessons.	

	WEEK I	WEEK II	WEEK III	WEEK IV
SEPT	Establishing discipline procedures. Running. Jumping. Rolling. Jumping over partner. Long, low bridges. Rolling over partner. Surfer. Space awareness.	Running. Jumping for height. Rolling over partner. Long, low bridges. Wheels. Balancing on hands. Jumping for distance. Game (5:201).	Running and leaping. Jumping over partner in high position. Walk on hands dragging legs. Wheels. Jumping for distance. Hand balancing. Game 2 (5:201)	Same as sixth grade, Week IV. Game (5:202)
OCT	Balance with partner. Balance on partner. Jumping in groups of three. Hand balancing. Wheels. Walk on hands dragging feet. Balance on one part of body—two parts—etc. Game (5:204)	New ways of balancing with partner. Relays involving skills practiced thus far. Football shuttle relay.	Boy team tug-of-war. Girl team tug-of-war. High jumping over stretched rope. Rolling over stretched rope. Game—Jump the shot. Crack about. Game 2 (5:218)	With partner do something different with rope. Game—Jump the Shot. Game—Tug-of-war. Game—Balance Tug-of-war (only one foot on ground) Game (5:209)
NOV	Pyramids. Groups of 6 or 7 design own (girls and boys separated). Apparatus. Leap on to picnic table; run and jump off for distance. Try something new on table. Game (6:538)	Balance on table. Get on and off table in a new way. Wheel across table. Cross table using only hands. Leap off table; land and roll. Tumbling—rolls.	Repeat table activities. Obstacle course including long distance running. Table and moving stunts (e.g. wheels) Tumbling—headstand.	Ball handling. Bounce ball while moving at different speeds. Volley ball with partner. Volley using any body part with partner. Bounce ball hard; jump and catch. Crack about. Create own games.
DEC	Get ball from ground to hands in new way. Throw ball against wall. Throw ball before it bounces twice. Head ball with partner. Bounce ball with different part of body. Bounce ball with foot. Games 1, 2, and 3 (5:181)	Repeat previous week. Throw ball overhand to partner. Repeat for distance. Bounce; pass to partner. Pass ball to partner in different way. Sit and lift ball between feet. Repeat—hands off floor. Games 1, 2, 3 (5:83)	Kick ball to partner. Partner stop kicked ball in some way other than a catch. Repeat for distance. Kick ball to partner in different way. Move ball using something other than hands. Game 1, 2, (5:228)	Repeat previous week. Toss ball as high as possible still being able to catch it. Strike ball to partner. Try many different body parts while striking to partner. Game (5:235)
JAN	Repeat all ball activities. In groups of 3, pass balls among players in different ways. Make new patterns. Demonstrate these. Free play using balls. Game 1 (5:232)	Game: Bombardment Game: Boundary Ball Relays using ball activities Soccer dribble	Game: Zone Soccer (boys and girls separately)	Game: Zone Soccer (change team makeup)

			Game 2 (5:174)	Game 1, 2 (5:179)
F E B	Jump ropes. Jumping individual ropes. Leaping individual ropes. Pepper. Jumping backward. Do a stunt while jumping. Move in a new way while jumping. With partner, one pull against rope held by stationary partner. Game (5:165) Create own games.	Repeat previous week. Jump with partner in different ways. Jump rope on to a box and off again. Hold rope tight in two hands; twist and stretch against tension. (Use Coke case for box.) Game (5:174)		
M A R	Choice Day Game (5:189)	Game—Keep Away Game—End Ball Game (5:194) Game—Around the World (shooting for basket) Free throw shooting contest.	Repeat games of previous weeks. Game—Captain Basketball—girls. Game (5:195)	Steal the flag.
A P R	Game—Captain Basketball Girls Game—Around the World Game (6:547)	Track and field. Hurdler 18", 24", or 30" Softball throwing for distance. 50 yard dash. 600 walk and run. Shuttle run—pull ups. Std. brd. jump.	Broad jump. High jump. Softball throw for accuracy. Soccer dribble. Game (6:541) Game (5:229)	Repeat track and field events. Track and field meet. (lower grades observe)
M A Y	Softball—boys Game 1, 2, 3 (5:248) Kickball—girls Volleyball serve Game (5:276)	Softball—boys Kickball—girls Volleyball—pass game (5:278)	Softball—boys Softball—girls Volleyball game (5:280)	Softball—boys Softball—girls Newcomb
J U N E	Coed—Hit Pin Soccer Free play One bounce volleyball game (5:283)	Coed—Steal the Flag Bombardment Choice Day	Note: Rhythms excellent rainy day work. Pole dancing enjoyed at this level. "Recess activities" good for free play days.	

	WEEK I	WEEK II	WEEK III	WEEK IV
SEPT	Establish discipline procedure. Running for speed and distance. Bridges. Hand balancing. Rolling. Leg Dragging. Jumping for heights and distance. Space Awareness	Repeat first week. Leaping. In groups of 3, jumping partners. Balancing with partners. Rolling with partners. Tumbling—head stands.	2 picnic tables: Leap onto table, run across, jump off. Jump off for height or distance. Get on table, roll across, get off in new way. Jump on table, cross, lie down and get off. Head stand. Tumbling—somersaults.	Repeat above. Go across table, jump off, land and roll. Do something new on table, get off backward. Cartwheel across tables. Tumbling—pyramid rolls.
OCT	Game (1:201) Repeat above. Horizontal ladder. Cross ladder using just hands. Cross ladder moving backward. Cross ladder using every other rung. Hang in a new way. Single rail—pass each other. Double rail—the same.	Repeat above. Dismount ladder in a new way. Lift self up on to ladder from center. Weave in and out of ladder rungs. Cross ladder using just one bar. Hang for 20 sec. Game (5:202)	Balls: Kicking for distance in different ways. Kick to partner. Dribble with feet. Stop kicked ball with feet. Stop kicked ball in another way not using hands. Game (5:204) Game (5:205)	Repeat above. Dribble ball and kick. With partner volley ball with head many times. Crack about. Game (5:223)
NOV	Soccer (boys and girls separate) Game—Zone Soccer Game (5:228)	Game—Zone Soccer (girls) Game (5:229)	Boys Football Game—Soccer Girls Game (5:232)	Game—Soccer Relays using soccer skills Choice Day
DEC	Balls: Bounce ball while moving at different speeds. Repeat, moving in different directions. Bounce at different levels. Jump over ball. Game (5:158)	Bounce ball hard—jump to catch ball rebound. Strike ball with fist to partner many times. Repeat for distance. Get ball from ground to hands without bending to use hands. (Game 5:160)	Repeat above. Sit and pick ball up with feet. Repeat and pass to partner's feet. Roll over ball. Drag body with ball between feet. Bounce ball with different part of body. Game 2 (5:160)	With partner volley ball back and forth with hands. Competition to see which pair can complete most volleys. Free play. Game 1, 2 (5:276)
JAN	Volleyball. Game—One Bounce Volleyball Game (5:278)	Game—One Bounce Volleyball Game (5:280)	One Bounce Volleyball Game (5:283) Game (5:283)	Coed Volleyball Volleyball Boys Game—Volleyball Volleyball Girls

FEB	Dance—Stick Dance Dances (5:295)	Dances (6:690-714)	Square dance or folk dance. Repeat above. Movement exploration rhythms.	Same Square dance or folk dance. Movement exploration rhythms.
MAR	Basketballs: Bouncing at different speeds in different directions. Passing to partner —one arm, chest pass, bounce pass, two hand overhead. Game 1, 2, 3 (5:181)	Game: In groups of 4—keep away. Foul shooting practice. Game: Twenty-One Game: Horse Games 1, 2, 3 (5:182)	Games 1, 2, 3 (5:176) Zone basketball Girls zone basketball	Game: Repeat previous week. Zone Basketball Girls zone basketball
APR	Game: Basketball (5:189) Game (5:190)	Game: Basketball Game (5:191)	Track: En masse—practice sprint start. Sprinting, long jumping, high jumping over stretched rope. Softball throw for distance. Softball throw for accuracy. Shuttle run.	Repeat above. Basketball throw for distance. 100 yd. dash. 600 yd. walk, run. Shot put. Leather covered shot. Std. broad jump.
MAY	Balls: Throw overhand for distance. With partner throw and catch for height. Roll and catch with partner. Game 1, 2, 3 (5:248)	Softball: Throwing for accuracy with partner. Throw for distance with partner. Catching high throws; catching rolled balls. Batting practice. Game 1, 2, 3 (5:250-51)	Softball. Game (5:265) Game (5:266)	Game—Softball Game (5:267)
JUNE	Game—Softball Game 2 (5:270)	Steal the flag. Choice Day	Note: "Recess Activities" are good free play games. Coed softball games	

Appendix

PRIMARY OBSTACLE COURSE

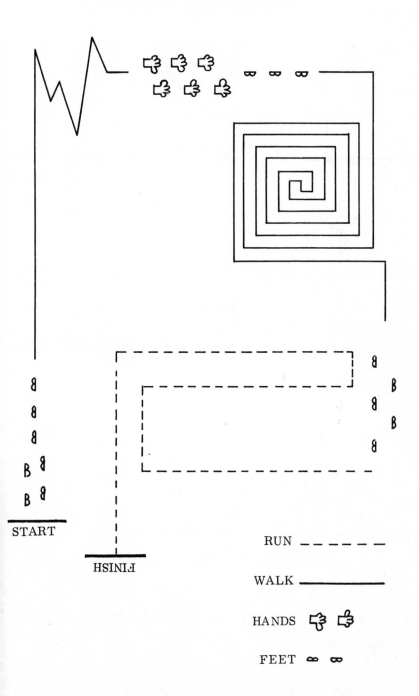

OBSTACLE COURSE – PRIMARY LEVEL

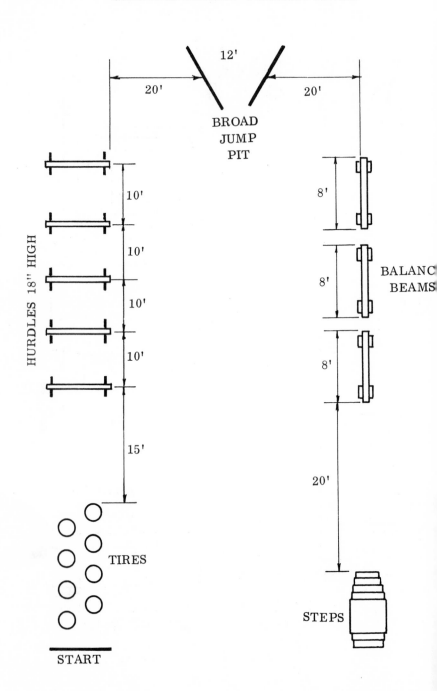

BLACK TOP PAINTED OBSTACLE COURSE

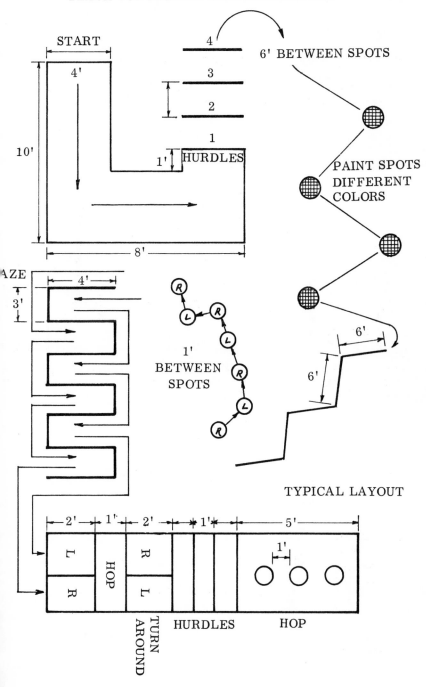

6' BETWEEN SPOTS

PAINT SPOTS
DIFFERENT
COLORS

1'
BETWEEN
SPOTS

TYPICAL LAYOUT

TRAINING STEPS

Dimensions and styles may vary with steps.

Steps should be at least one foot deep, two feet wide

Rails are not necessary but helpful in Primary Grades.
Also rails add utility to the challenges that can be given.

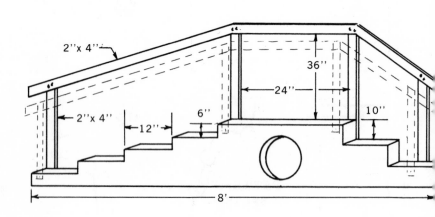

TEACHING SUGGESTIONS

1.   Can you touch each step?

2.   Who can touch every other step?

3.   Can you go across without touching any steps?

4.   Who can go through each rail opening?

ALANCE BEAM

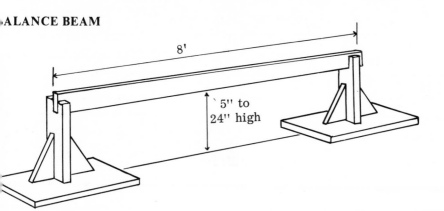

8'

5" to
24" high

- May be purchased.
- May be made according to needs of children
- Beam is 2 x 4 removable so that different sides can be used.

ALANCE BOARD

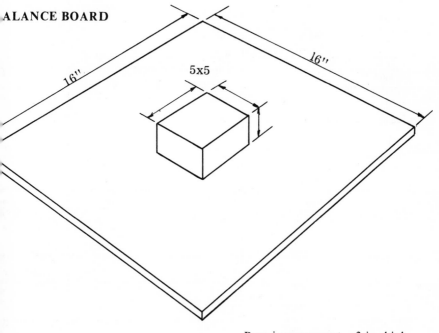

16"

16"

5x5

Base is permanent — 3 in. high
5 x 5
4 x 4
3 x 3

xterior grade plywood or similar material

	No. Equip.	Balls	Hoops	Jump Ropes
STRENGTH 1.	Bridges, high & low. Balancing. Jumping. Hopping. Leaping. Partner support. Transport body on hands. Sprinting.	Volleying. Carry ball between feet. Use feet to toss ball. Jump over ball. Jump to catch. Throw for distance, kick for same.	Tossing. Catching. Spinning. Jumping over. Diving through.	Tug-O-War. Jumping rope. Skipping rope. Jumping over rope f height.
ENDURANCE 2.	Hopping. Jumping. Leaping. Running. Skipping. Galloping. Dodging.	Skip while bouncing. Run while bouncing. Jump & catch. Rebound. Volleying.	Roll, catch. Throw, run, catch. Roll, dive through. Run, leap over hoop obstacle. Jump or hop through hoop obstacle.	Jump for time. Consecutive jumps. foot. Alternate feet. Run while jumping.
FLEXIBILITY 3.	Rolling. Bridges. Twisting. Dodging. Balance. Make self large or small. Moving about stationary body part. Shadow patterns.	Go low while bouncing. Low, high. Toss, turn, catch. Drop catch. Ball around self. Around back to back. Roll over ball without touching.	Dive through. Throw high & catch. Step in & out, over & under. Lift hoop with feet. Spin hoop.	Cross rope over and jumps high & low. T Bend low. Touch gro Pull rope with partne Turn while keeping r taut.
AGILITY 4.	Obstacle run. Space orientation. Dodging. Moving from high to low. Start: Stop. Roll. Move on 3-4-5 support points.	Dodge each other while bouncing. Jump, turn, catch. Roll, run, catch. Drop catch. Circling dropped ball.	Roll, run around. Hoops on ground, dodge in and out. Leap in, leap out. Jump in, out of spinning hoop.	Double ropes. Boxe shuffle. Partners, s rope. Reverse in, ou Jump touch heels.
BALANCE 5.	One foot stand, low & high. Leaping. Inverted positions. Hopping. Partner support. Starting, stopping. Reaching.	Balance ball on body. Hopping over ball. Bouncing while on one foot.	Stand on one foot hold hoop over head. On one hand. Hop in and out of hoop.	Rope on ground: Jump touch toe. Jun touch ground. Jump kick forward. Hop ro Move along rope usi just hands.
SPEED 6.	Hopping. Leaping. Jumping. Galloping. Stopping, starting. Running.	Dribble with foot. Dribble with hand. Passing to partner. Rolling & chasing ball.	Run, catch rolling hoop.	Jumping rope. Hopping rope. Skipping rope. Pepp
HAND EYE COORDINATION 7.		Ball bouncing. Toss & catch. Bounce & catch. Drop & catch. Volleying. Striking.	Toss, run, catch. Roll with hand. Backspin & catch hoop. Tossing hoop & looping it over arm.	Rope around in rhyt
FOOT EYE COORDINATION 8.		Kick stationary & moving ball. Punt ball. Kick bouncing ball. Soccer dribble. Feet to hands.	Roll with foot. Step in & out of hoops. Obstacle course.	Jump single rope. J double rope. Jump alternate feet. Jum swinging rope by pa
CREATIVITY 9.	Bridges, partners. Balance new ways. Wheels. Body contortions. Move to rhythm. Express a mood. Shadows. Invent games.	Bouncing: with other body parts. Pass in groups of 3. Rhythm. Turning. Clap. Invent games or routines.	Roll, go through a new way. Take body through hoop. Throw hoop to partner. Spin clockwise. Invent games.	Turn around making different shapes wi rope, partner. Turn Invent games & rou
RHYTHMS 10.	Gliding, clapping, moving body parts, slow motion, name or rhythm sounds. Swinging, stomping. Move to beat. Questions & answers.	Bounce to rhythm. Throw to partner. Pass around group. Skip while bouncing.	Hoop on ground—jump in, jump out while clapping. Twist or turn with hoop.	Chanting rhythm of rhymes—swinging i
SPATIAL ORIENTATION 11.	Step to empty space. Walk or run to space. Inverted position. Lateral, forward, backward movement. Dodging. Change body position. Jump to target.	Bounce to new spot. Return to old. Skip to new spot. Run, dodge. Throw at target. Volley at target. Kick at target.	Hoops on ground—jump in, front, side, rear. Jump in forward. Jump out backward. Jump out sideways.	Jump high, jump lo Jump sideways. Jur back and forth. Tw & turning.
SOCIAL INTERACTION 12.		WORKING WITH PARTNER OR IN		

atons (Wands)	Bamboo Poles	Tires	Innertube	Flash Cards
wrestle. Diving batons. Leaping batons. Jumping batons.	Pair pulling.	Jump on rims. Leap over tires. Run around rolling tire. Lift tire overhead, throw.	Jump on, bounce off. Roll with person inside. Tu-O-War. Passing tube overhead to partner.	Hopping to pattern. Jumping to pattern. Running to pattern. (i.e. square, zig-zag, circle …)
	Tinikling (pole dance). Partner routine.	Obstacle run. Run, catch rolling tire. Pushing & chasing tire.	Rolling. Jump on rim. Roll and chase. Roll, run & catch, run around. Tug-O-War.	Sustained activity. Jumping, hopping, certain shapes.
ing to maintain nce of wand. sting to keep balance. d on both ends to e around body.	Tinikling (pole dance). High, low movements. Crawling between parallel lying poles. Moving on hands & feet under crossed poles.	Dodging patterns. Run around several tires. Vault over rolling tire. Fit inside tire to be rolled by partner.	Leap-on, twist off. Crawl in and out of tube. Fit inside while partner rolls.	Running, jumping, hopping patterns. Shape body to patterns.
ing to keep balance. nging sticks with ner. Turning while k balances. Jumping baton for height.	Tinikling. High, low. Various dance patterns.	One foot in, out. Jump in, out. Land on tire-off. Leap in, out. One foot in, step to next tire, knees high. Vault rolling tire.	Bounce several times, feet to knees. Sit bounce.	Running to right, left. Turning, leaping, hopping, jumping, skipping.
nce on body parts, ers, horizontal arm, , nose, foot, hand.	Tinikling. Hopping. Jumping. Step in and out.	Vault over rolling tire. Leap, land on tire side, off. Hop through obstacle course. Balance on upright tire. Walk on rim.	Bounce. Leap. Jump on tube. Ride like horse.	Leaping. Running right & left. Hopping. Jumping.
around balancing on. Changing anced baton with ner. Turn around ch balanced baton.	Foot in, foot out. Straddle jump. Move from one pole to another.	Run through pattern for time. Roll & chase tire. Roll tire, run around it.	Roll tube, run & catch. Roll tube, run around it.	Running patterns. Hopping. Stopping, starting.
ance on hand. ance on fingers. ssing vertical poles partners.		Rolling tire with hand. Catch rolling tire, stop with hand.	Throw at rolling target. Throw at stationary target.	
lance on foot vertical. lance on foot rizontal. Stepping long crossed batons.	Tinikling. Foot in, foot out. Alternate-steps.	Roll tire by using feet. Jump in center. Leap in center. Skip around tire. Obstacle course.	Jump on. Leap on. Alternate foot hop.	
ange with partner. row to. Pass to in cle. Jump over. lance on stick. Balance ay. Invent games.	Tinikling. Change rhythm. Partner follow the leader. Devise own routine— single, partner, with a ball. Invent games.	Change obstacle patterns. Work with partner use balls. Stack tires. Invent games.	Free bouncing. Roll with partner. Invent games.	Run name in script. Lightning, Corkscrew, Big Cloud, Checkers. Invent games.
oup rhythm pass. nging batons to ythm. Pass batons to rtner.	Tinikling. Change rhythm using creative ideas.	Jump on tires to beat or rhythm. Stepping in and out of tire to rhythm.		Move to rhythm.
ass to side. Move to ew space while alancing. Move among attered batons.	Up, down, in, out. High, low.	Around, on, up, down, through.	Up, down, off, on, in, out, through.	In & out. Right, left. Forward, backward.

SMALL GROUPS IN ABOVE ACTIVITIES

	Balance Beam	Balance Board	Incline Board	Hurdles
STRENGTH 1.	Balance on foot. Balance on hands & feet. Balance on seat.	One leg stand. Two leg stand. Balance while bouncing. Balance while passing ball to partner.	Balance board while standing. Hop up board & down other side. Jump up board & down other side.	Jumping over. Leaping over. Diving over. Crawling under.
ENDURANCE 2.	Sustain low balanced position.		Hopping up board. Jumping up board.	Run distance.
FLEXIBILITY 3.	Turning, squatting. One foot stand. Hands & feet.	Knee bend to maintain balance. Bend forward, sideways or backward to catch ball. Squat low. Stand high.	Knee bend to maintain balance. Balance while standing. Crawl up & down board. Roll down board.	Leg over high hurdle, low hurdle. Crawling under. Going over & under alternately.
AGILITY 4.	Turning. Reverse heel toe. Short leaps. Cross beam using hands and feet.	Bend to keep balance. Reach for high toss. Reach for low toss. Reach for wide toss.	Keep board in balanced position.	Leap and jump over. Dive over. Crawl under.
BALANCE 5.	Heel-toe forward, backward. Heel-toe one foot. Change direction. Pass. Squat low, rise.	One foot stand, two foot. Bounce ball. Balance on one foot. Toss to partner. Toss & catch (self). Toss, clap, catch. Squat low.	Moving incline up & down. Maintain balanced position. Balance board with partner. Hop or jump up & down board.	Leaping over. Hopping over.
SPEED 6.				Clear hurdles for time. Jumping, leaping, hopping. Crawling under quickly.
HAND EYE COORDINATION 7.	Bend touch bar with hands.	Bouncing to self. Bounce to partner. Toss to self. Toss to partner.		
FOOT EYE COORDINATION 8.	Heel-toe balance. Hopping. Skipping.			Hopping over. Leaping over. Jumping over.
CREATIVITY 9.	Pass partner. Alternate feet. Different short leaps. Invent games.	Move board by manipulating feet. Bounce ball around. Partner groups-ball pass, toss. Invent games	Make up routine. Balance objects. Invent games.	Arrange own obstacle course. Invent games.
RHYTHMS 10.	In time to music. In time to clapping. Getting on, stopping, turning, getting off.	Bounce to music. Bounce to partner in rhythm.	Roll back & forth to rhythm.	
SPATIAL ORIENTATION 11.	Leap up. Jump down. Balance forward. Balance sideways. Bend back.	High, side, low, back.	Balance point.	Go over different heights. Go under different heights.
SOCIAL INTERACTION 12.		WORKING WITH PARTNER OR IN		

Stairs	Tables	Horizontal Ladders	Turn Bars	Stilts
g on each stair. g on each stair. ng across using rossing using nly.	Vault on. Pull self across. Jump off for height or distance. Get on new way. Drag self under.	Hanging. Cross using arms, on single or double rail. Weaving in & out of bars. Hanging & raising legs. Pull-ups.	Forward turn over bar. Reverse turn under. Skin the cat. Hanging, moving across using just hands.	Walking on stilts— Forward, backward, sideways.
g across stairs. g across stairs. g quickly across Crossing using nly.		Hanging, travel across moving forward, sideways or backward. Swinging.	Routine on bar.	Increase distance to walk. Walk obstacle course. Walk up & down stairs.
along rails using & feet. Crawling t of uprights. ng over & rails.	Climb onto table. Crawl off, under. Roll across. Slide off from lying position. Jump off, touch knees with hands.	Weave in & out of rungs. Swinging until toes touch bars. Crawling across using hands & legs to cross under. Skin the cat.	Turns. Sloth across. Skin the cat. Forward turn over bar. Reverse turn under.	Step over rope. Balance on stilts without stepping.
ng quickly on every opping or jumping y stair. Move ails using hands & se arms only.	Vaulting on, leaping off, landing & rolling. Rolling across, crawling under for speed.	Travel across. Go across using hands & feet. Travel, skipping rungs forward & backward.	Vaults over low bar. Sloth across. Move across top.	Maintain balance while still or moving. Using stilts on hop scotch pattern.
er steps. Walk s. Stand on rails. ail.	Hopping across. Vaulting on. Jumping & turning off. Inverted position on table.	Standing on top. Going across top of ladder. Inverted hang.	Sit on top. Go across top using hands & legs.	Balance feet even, feet spread. Balance without stepping. Stunts on stilts. Walking a line forward, backward & sideways.
un, hop or jump stairs. Use arms ong rails-moving .	Going across table as quickly as possible. Going under as quickly as possible.	Traveling across quickly. Slothing across quickly.		Racing on stilts. Slalom course. Stepping over ropes quickly.
uickly across each Hop across each	Leap to table top.			Lift stilts to move through obstacle course. Go up & down stairs.
d stairs are ship, ain, fort, etc. for e play. games.	New ways for getting on, going across & getting off. Invent stunts for top of table. Invent games.	Going across new ways. Hanging in new ways. Doing new stunts. Invent games.	Individual free routines. New ways to hang. Invent games.	Invent stunts on stilts. Invent games.
			Free movement to rhythmic choice.	March on stilts.
& out of uprights. er & under rails.	Jump or leap on. Jump off & over obstacle. Crawl under.	Weaving in & out of rungs. Drop from ladder onto feet.	Around, up, down, over, under, swing, turn.	Adjust to height & length of stilts. Go under high rope.

SMALL GROUPS IN ABOVE ACTIVITIES

Bibliography

Laban, Rudolf and F. C. Lawrence. EFFORT. London: McDonald and Evans, 1950.

Kephart, Newell C. THE SLOW LEARNER IN THE CLASSROOM. Columbus: Charles E. Merrill Books, Inc., 1964.

SUGGESTED READINGS

1. Anderson, Marian H., Margaret E. Elliot, and Jeanne La Berge. PLAY WITH A PURPOSE. New York and London: Harper and Row, Publishers, 1966.

2. Mosston, Muska. TEACHING PHYSICAL EDUCATION From Command to Discovery. Columbus: Charles E. Merrill Books, Inc., 1966.

3. Mosston, Muska. DEVELOPMENTAL MOVEMENT. Columbus: Charles E. Merrill Books, Inc., 1965.

4. Kephart, Newell C. THE SLOW LEARNER IN THE CLASSROOM. Columbus: Charles E. Merrill Books, Inc., 1964.

5. Nagel, Charles and Fredericka Moore. SKILL DEVELOPMENT THROUGH GAMES AND RHYTHMIC ACTIVITIES. Palo Alto, California: The National Press, 1966.

6. Van Hagen, Winifred, Genevie Dexter and Jesse Feiring Williams. PHYSICAL EDUCATION IN THE ELEMENTARY SCHOOL. Sacramento: California State Department of Education, 1951.